REMEMBER RENO

A Biography
Of
Major General Jesse Lee Reno

Major General Jesse Lee Reno
Massachusetts Commandery Military
Order of the Loyal Legion and the
U.S. Military History Institute

REMEMBER RENO

A Biography
Of
Major General Jesse Lee Reno

By
William F. McConnell

 White Mane Publishing Co., Inc.

This White Mane publication was printed by
Beidel Printing House, Inc.
63 West Burd Street
Shippensburg, PA 17257 USA

In respect for the scholarship contained herein, the acid-free paper
used in this book meets the guidelines for permanence and durability of
the Committee on Production Guidelines for Book Longevity of the Council on Library Resources.

For a complete list of available publications please write:
White Mane Publishing Company, Inc.
P.O. Box 152
Shippensburg, PA 17257 USA

Library of Congress Cataloging-in-Publication Data

McConnell, William F., 1921–
    Remember Reno : a biography of Major General Jesse Lee Reno/ by
William F. McConnell.
        p.   cm.
    Includes bibliographical references and index.
    ISBN 1-57249-020-9 (alk. paper)
    1. Reno, Jesse Lee, 1823–1862. 2. Generals--United States-
-Biography. 3. United States. Army--Biography. 4. United
States--History--Civil War, 1861–1863--Campaigns.   I. Title.
E467.1.R36M37   1996
973.7'42'092--dc20
[B]   96-16506
                                                            CIP

PRINTED IN THE UNITED STATES OF AMERICA

To Louise

Helpmate and inspiration

in all aspects of this work

CONTENTS

Introduction x
      Highlights of Life
      Confused with Marcus Reno

1. Reno Roots 1
      Brief Family History
      Birth in Wheeling
      Youth in Franklin, Pa.

2. Cadet Reno 4
      To West Point in 1842 – Part of the famous
          Class of 1846
      Graduated July 1, 1846

3. Young Lieutenants Off To War 8
      Reno's participation in the War with Mexico
      Two brevet promotions for "Gallant and
          Meritorious Conduct"

4. Peacetime In The Regular Army 16
      Service in Washington, D.C.
      Meets Future Wife
      Surveys New Road in Minnesota
      Duty at Frankfort Arsenal

5. When The Saints Went Marching 24
      Two-Year Duty in Utah
      The Letters of Mary Reno

6. Mount Vernon And Fort Leavenworth 36
      Commands Arsenals at Both of the Above
      Civil War Breaks Out

7. With Burnside In North Carolina 42
      Promoted to Brigadier General
      Distinguishes Himself in North Carolina Campaign

8. With Pope In Virginia 56
      Promoted to Major General
      Does Well in Second Battle of Bull Run

9. The Battle Of Chantilly 64
      His Troops Halt "Stonewall" Jackson

10. The Road To Frederick 70
       Feud with Rutherford B. Hayes
       Meeting with Barbara Fritchie and Receiving
          Flag from Her
11. Touched By Fate 76
       Lee's Famous "Lost Order"
       Reno Leads Union Force at Battle of South Mountain
       Gen. Reno Killed
       Speculation on Whose Bullet Caused His
          Death—Friend or Foe's
12. Our True And Loved Commander 88
       Tributes to Reno
       Noted Achievements of Two Sons
       Monument Dedication in 1889 and
          100th Anniversary Rededication in 1989

Notes 97
Bibliography 105
Index 110

ACKNOWLEDGEMENTS

I have been fortunate to have had the aid and support of a number of people in accomplishing this work. Foremost among them is my mentor, Michael J. Brodhead, professor emeritus of the University of Nevada, Reno, who provided me guidance in most every phase of this endeavor. I offer my sincere gratitude also to attorney Roger Reno for his guidance, encouragement and extensive Reno family genealogy.

I am indebted and give sincere thanks to the many others who assisted me in gathering source material. Among them are: George Brigham, Jr.; Steven R. Stotelmyer; Colonel William Willmann; Diana Murar; Charles Davis; the staff of the Franklin, Pennsylvania Historical Society; Anne Hawkins of the Washoe County Public Library, Reno, Nevada; my son, Timothy S. McConnell; Diane McConnell; my daughter Carley A. Smith; Clyde Johnson; and Mary Jane Powell, Jesse Reno's grand-niece. Special gratitude is extended to my editor, Martin K. Gordon, Ph. D., for his professional guidance in the final preparation of this biography.

INTRODUCTION

On the bloodiest single day of the American Civil War, northern troops of the IX Corps, struggling to cross Antietam Creek at Burnside Bridge, rallied to the name of their newly fallen leader with the cry of: "Remember Reno". Their commander, Major General Jesse Lee Reno, had lost his life while leading them in battle at South Mountain, Maryland just three days earlier on September 14, 1862. Who then was this man who could elicit such great admiration from others, and would posterity "Remember Reno"?

Jesse Reno was a brilliant officer, a stern but highly respected leader and a hero in two of America's wars. He led troops that possibly saved our nation's capital and even the Union itself. He was associated with three future presidents, two of whom were under his war-time command. One of these drew sufficient wrath from Reno to cause him to threaten to put the man in irons. How history may have been changed had he court-martialed that officer-politician gives rise to much fanciful speculation. Reno's in-laws included men of great prominence. His father-in-law had been a nationally honored military martyr and his wife's grandfather had inspired the writing of the National Anthem. Two of Jesse Reno's sons became famous, one as a lawyer and the other as the inventor of one of our daily-used modern conveniences. Together, these two sons introduced one of our more popular sports to the United States. Several coincidences intertwined his life with that of his good friend and later battlefield enemy, Thomas Jonathan "Stonewall" Jackson. Some have even compared the circumstances of their deaths to suggest that Jesse Reno was killed by his own men. He was a beloved husband and father whose life reflected no hint of moral laxity or personal shortcoming. He was proclaimed by many of his nationally known contemporaries as one of the best military leaders around at the time.

All of the above would seem to be the attributes of a well-known person—the prerequisites of lasting fame and a name that would come easily to the tongues of almost everyone. However, it was not to be and the light of his fame would glow for only a brief time. In the present day, Jesse Lee Reno is all but forgotten except for a few diligent Civil War scholars and researchers.

If any one reason could be singled out for the shunting of Jesse Lee Reno out of the limelight of history, it would seem to be the stigma that many inaccurately associate with his last name. More often than not, this writer has found that when he has mentioned that he was researching the life of Jesse Reno, the response has been in the nature of: "Oh, you mean the fellow who let Custer down at the Little Big Horn". It would appear that for much of our population, the only association with the name, Reno, has been with the Custer massacre. The officer who served there with Custer was Major Marcus Albert Reno, a man only distantly related to Jesse Reno. Whether rightly or wrongly accused of contributing to the Little Big Horn fiasco, Marcus Reno, through succeeding years, has accumulated widespread notoriety. It is unfortunate for Jesse Reno's reputation that he is frequently confused with Marcus and the cloud of infamy has mistakenly fallen on him.

The following, therefore, is an attempt to illuminate the unsung and often overlooked accomplishments of a true American hero— Major General Jesse Lee Reno. The relative brevity of this account of his life is due to the near lack of surviving records of the family which were pertinent to his private life. At one time, family records were accumulated by a daughter-in-law, but these appear to have been lost or destroyed after her death in 1955. An extensive search of logical sources of biographical information, over more than seven years, as well as contact with nearest surviving relatives, have failed to reveal further details of the private life of Jesse Lee Reno.

1 — RENO ROOTS

Few of us can claim more extensive American ancestry than Jesse Lee Reno. Born in 1823, he was a fifth generation American-born Reno. The first of his lineage to come to this country was Lewis Reynaud. As his name would indicate, Lewis was born in France circa 1676. As a boy he immigrated to London, England in 1688 and then, when about twenty-four, he continued on to America in 1700.

Through the years following Lewis Reynaud's immigration to America, confusion has arisen concerning the original spelling of the family name. Most published biographical sketches state that Jesse Reno's name came from the French "Renault". However, records do not indicate that any of his American ancestors ever used this spelling, even as an alternate. As with many European names that for convenience would become anglisized in America, Lewis Reynaud's descendants would try a variety of simplified spellings that would provide essentially the same sound as the French name. Even Lewis himself is reported to have used both "Renoe" and "Reno". Others of the clan would follow with: Renno, Rennoe, Reneau and Rayno. But overall, the phonetically simple "Reno" would win out among the bulk of Lewis Reynaud's descendants.

Originally, Lewis Reno settled in Prince William County, Virginia. This area, south and west of Alexandria, now has as its county seat the town of Manassas. It also includes among its natural features a creek known as Bull Run. That Lewis selected this particular area might seem almost prophetic, for his illustrious descendant, Jesse, would distinguish himself more than a century and a half later while leading the Union army's IX Corps over the same terrain during the Second Battle of Bull Run. Little else is recorded regarding the life and activities of Lewis Reno. His wife's name is unknown, as is their place of marriage. It would seem likely that he did not marry until coming to this country, for the first of his five children was not born until 1702, two years after his emigration. We know that Lewis Reno sired at least four sons and a daughter before dying in 1754. The youngest son, John, married Susanna Thorn and they were to continue the lineage that would lead to Jesse Lee Reno.[1]

As with many early emigrant families, Jesse's antecedents pushed farther west into the new lands, ever searching for their elusive Garden of Eden as each might perceive it. John Reno lived for a time at Winchester, Virginia, then moved on to Patterson Creek in what is now the eastern edge of West Virginia. Subsequently, John would move north to an area near present day Pittsburgh to join his son, Benjamin, an early settler at Chartier Creek. Possibly the Renos had been drawn to that area by other Frenchmen who were settling around Fort Duquesne. With the advent of the French and Indian War, French dominance was cut short. By 1758, Fort Duquesne had fallen to British military forces and the Reno family migration continued farther north and west. In 1798, Jesse Reno's grandfather, Charles and his wife Frances Laughlin, became early settlers of Sharon, a town on the northwestern border of Pennsylvania. There, Jesse's father, Lewis Thomas, was born in 1795. He married Rebecca Quinby and, in their search for a place to put down roots, Lewis and Rebecca lived for a time in Wheeling, Virginia (now West Virginia). During that sojourn, Jesse Lee Reno was born on April 20, 1823. He was the third oldest of the eight children of Lewis and Rebecca.[2]

At the time of Jesse Reno's death, thirty-nine years later, his battlefield opponent, Confederate General D. H. Hill, would somewhat disdainfully accuse Reno of having been a "renegade Virginian"; the assertion being that he had deserted his native southern homeland and heritage.[3] This was far from the truth, for in no sense was Jesse Reno ever a "southerner". Though born in Wheeling at a time when it was in western Virginia, the great majority of the people there would show their allegiance to the North at the outbreak of the Civil War. They broke away from Virginia to create their own state of West Virginia and remained loyal to the Union. Further, Jesse was barely seven years old when his parents moved back to their native Pennsylvania, and thus he had no true "southern heritage".

In 1830, young Jesse's father had learned of a business boom around Franklin, Pennsylvania which was spurred by the building of an extension of the Erie Canal. His parents, Lewis and Rebecca, moved the family to Franklin, where the father operated a hotel in the heart of the town on the corner of Otter and 13th Street (now a bank parking lot).[4] This pleasant western Pennsylvania community, with its timbered hills and beautiful Allegheny River, surely would have provided an ideal setting for the formulative years of young Jesse. The hotel was a block or so from the river and there must have been many enticing diversions for the inquisitive and playful boy. Significantly, and whether by design or not, most of the places Jesse would reside in the remainder of his life would be in homes that overlooked large rivers.

While Jesse's twelve years in Franklin doubtless contained many pleasurable events, all was not totally a happy time for the boy. One can imagine the deep sorrow experienced by the ten-year-old lad on a September day in 1833 when a younger brother, Wilford, was being lowered into his grave at the back of the old Pioneer Cemetery. Years later Jesse would honor his lost brother by giving his youngest son the middle name of Wilford.

An early history of the area states the following: "In boyhood Jesse L. Reno was of handsome countenance, of medium stature, brave and quick in action, and a generous companion."[5]

Schooling for Jesse, for that time, could be considered good and he appears to have had the benefit of fine instructors. Among the teachers in Franklin then were a Mr. Magill, a graduate of Jefferson College; Cyrus Nutt, a graduate of Allegheny College and the Reverend Nathaniel R. Snowmen. Also, one of Jesse's teachers was a Mr. Gamble, a Scotch-Irishman who was described as "rather peculiar in his ways and appearance". Gamble was a fine linguist and mathematician and young Reno did quite well under his tutelage.[6] Jesse's education in Franklin would serve him well when he entered the U.S. Military Academy at West Point in 1842.

$2-$ CADET RENO

Jesse Reno's departure from Franklin in the summer of 1842 marked the end of his civilian life. From West Point cadet to the Civil War, he would remain on active military duty until his death. In this he differed from many of his classmates and other military academy graduates who, after varying periods of service, resigned their commissions to pursue civilian occupations until the eruption of the Civil War.

Jesse's parents, brothers and sisters also were destined to move from Franklin in a short span of time. In 1848 they had moved to Erie, Pennsylvania and then subsequently to Chicago. Brothers Lewis and Benjamin went on to Marengo, Iowa, where they both became prominent merchants. Parents Lewis and Rebecca also moved to Marengo and Jesse's father died there in 1870. His mother then moved back east to Cambridge, Massachusetts, to live with a daughter, Mrs. Rebecca Eliot.[1]

One can but wonder what the Reno family fortunes might have been had they stayed in Franklin for a while longer. In another decade or so after their departure, history was made a short distance away when the world's first oil well was drilled at Titusville in August of 1859. Franklin and the surrounding area became engulfed in the resulting oil boom. By the mid-1860s a small community had grown up about four miles to the north which was established in support of the oil industry and it was named Reno. This village was also a terminus for the short-lived and short-line Reno, Oil Creek and Pithole Railroad. It existed as a freight line for only a few months between 1864 and 1866.[2] The village of Reno still exists but has dwindled in population since reaching its peak around 1871–1872.

When Jesse joined the Class of 1846 at West Point he looked forward to new-found friendships and camaraderie with fellow cadets. He likely had no thought that the then festering North-South rivalry and bitterness would one day pit them against each other in deadly combat. Many of those young plebes of the summer of 1842 were destined to achieve high rank and fame in the coming mortal struggle. Some, like Jesse Reno, would sacrifice their lives for the causes that they each believed righteous.

Of the Class of '46, Major General Orlando B. Willcox, a number of years after the Civil War, would comment: "It was not considered a first-rate class, and by no means equal to that which preceded them. But they turned out as bright a galaxy of names as any class that ever graduated from the Military Academy."[3] They produced a number of noted Civil War generals, a presidential candidate, several governors, a renowned humorist-author and several men who could and would be considered heroes in their own time.

Leading the pack in later life, and nearly so as a cadet, was George B. McClellan, a talented young man from Philadelphia. A brilliant but sometimes irresolute commander McClellan would twice head the Union forces during the war and then would unsuccessfully challenge Lincoln for his second term as president. In later life, he served as governor of New Jersey. Cadet McClellan graduated second in his class at West Point.

Not nearly as brilliant academically as McClellan was Cadet George Edward Pickett, famed for leading a doomed charge at Gettysburg. A Virginian, he chose to fight for the South during the Civil War. Pickett graduated at the bottom of his class at the military academy.

The Class of '46 had its own comedian, in the form of the irrepressible George H. Derby. After graduation, he served well in the Mexican War. Later, as a topographical engineer, he would be noted for his exploration of the lower Colorado River. Derby, unlike many of his classmates who became generals and politicians, gained his fame as humorist, under the pen name of John Phoenix. When a West Point professor once asked him the proper course of action as a commander of a besieged fort that would surely fall in forty-five days, Derby replied, "I would march out, let the enemy in, and at the end of forty-five days, I would change places with him." Many years later while exploring the navigability of the Colorado River up to Yuma, Arizona, Derby is reported to have said that a villainous soldier who died there and went straight to hell telegraphed back for his blankets!⁴ Seventh in final class standing Derby immediately preceded Jesse Reno. He also preceded Reno in death by one year, when he died in New York City in 1861 at the age of 38.⁵

There were many others in the class who would achieve fame as generals during the coming war that would pit friend against friend: men whose names were George Stoneman (USA), Darius Couch (USA), William Gardner (CSA), Alfred Gibbs (USA), Dabney Maury (CSA) and George Gordon (USA). This stellar group of future Civil War leaders also included Samuel D. Sturgis who, in 1862, would be recipient of some of the last words Jesse Lee Reno would utter: "Halloo, Sam, I'm dead!"⁶

Not to be overlooked in this array of friends and classmates was the young man who likely achieved the most fame of all during the Civil War. Surpassed only by Robert E. Lee as the most revered of Confederate commanders, Thomas Jonathan Jackson would gain renown under the name "Stonewall". The star-crossed lives of Jesse Reno and Tom Jackson and the comparisons made of the two could easily be the format for fictional stories of the Civil War era. Both young men were of Class of '46, and both were born in the region that would become the state of West Virginia. Both would achieve military rank very near the top of their respective armies, and each would be killed early in the war. Both also would be associated with the name "Stonewall": Jackson with it as a nickname and Reno, by having commanded the "Stonewall Regiment". Likewise, both would be inexorably tied to the famed Barbara Fritchie flag, Reno by fact and Jackson by legend. They would meet in battle and on two significant occasions their troops would directly oppose each other. A few romanticists and historians would carry the comparison even to the deaths of both men by claiming that each was shot by his own troops.⁷ But, even if we follow the more commonly accepted account that Jesse Reno was indeed killed by enemy fire, we would note that the Confederates were led by "Stonewall" Jackson's brother-in-law, Daniel Harvey Hill.

"I remember him quite well as a cadet. The same unassuming, quiet, but resolute and ambitious character in embryo, rather playful in disposition, he loved his joke, his studies and his classmates...." Thus General Orlando B. Willcox (USMA 1847) later described the young man, Jesse Reno.⁸ Certainly, while at the academy, Reno was not a martinet and his playful nature was, in part, reflected by the number of demerits he accrued—131 in all.⁹ Most of his gigs were for minor infractions which drew only one or two demerits each. During his first two years he was often caught laughing or otherwise being inattentive in ranks. His final two years saw less of the frivolously gained demerits and were more the result of lax housekeeping. From the standpoint of discipline, Cadet Reno had his biggest problems in his final year at West Point. During the summer encampment between his junior and senior years, he received his first major penalty on August 1 for "his disobedience of orders in not taking his seat when ordered". For this he received eight demerits and was deprived of some privileges for the remainder of the encampment. Two weeks later, he and George Stoneman were confined to the Guard Tent for a week. Jesse, as the senior officer of the guard, had neglected his duty by not stopping some "improper conduct" by other cadets at the guard tent. This infraction brought him four more demerits.[10] During the remainder of his time at the academy Jesse Reno generally stayed within the confines of cadet rules until June 13, 1846, when he was cited for being "out of quarters after taps" (8 demerits).[11] The proximity of this transgression to graduation might give cause to believe that "a bunch of the boys were whooping it up" in a premature celebration of their completion of the rigors of the academy.

July 1, 1846 was graduation day and Jesse Lee Reno was commissioned brevet second lieutenant in the Ordnance Corps. He was eighth in his class of 59 members and was the 1279th to graduate from the U.S. Military Academy.[12]

3— Young Lieutenants Off to War

Of the war with Mexico, 1846–1848, United States commander, General Winfield Scott said:

> "I give it as my fixed opinion that but for our graduated cadets the war between the United States and Mexico might, and probably would, have lasted some four or five years, with, in its first half, more defeats than victories falling to our share, whereas in two campaigns we conquered a great country and a peace without the loss of a single battle or skirmish."[1]

Thus, the Class of 1846 went off to war, most to gain laurels, and Lt. Jesse Reno was not to be omitted when tributes were later handed out for meritorious service. The names of so many young captains and lieutenants in the conflict with Mexico would become household words during another war a decade and a half later: Grant, Lee, Beauregard, McClellan, Meade, Bragg and others who were destined for high command during the Civil War. It has been stated that for the first time in an American war, the skill of the junior officers was commensurate with the bravery of the soldiers, that "the performance of ... the junior officers was encouraging" and, "...especially true of that technical arm, the artillery, and of the new mobile batteries."[2]

For Jesse Reno however, the Mexican War was, in a sense, fortuitous in that it provided the young academy graduate with career opportunities not likely otherwise available. Just a few years before the war, prospects for promotion were bleak because the army was barely growing and promotion was by seniority within a regiment or staff department. Frequently, and obviously in the case of Jesse Reno, vacancies in the rank of second lieutenant were too few to absorb new academy graduates. Thus they were often initially given brevet ranks and assigned more or less menial or specially created jobs.[3] Lieutenant Reno was spared this distasteful fate. Upon graduation, Reno was immediately assigned to be an assistant ordnance officer at the Watervliet Arsenal in New York. This assignment would soon be superseded by orders to go to Mexico with General Scott's force.[4]

Fortune smiled on young Lt. Reno in battle for he was to find himself well adapted to the relatively new technique of waging war— namely of utilizing high mobility in all branches of the American army, especially the artillery. To a major degree, warfare was being revolutionized. Reno was in the midst of the fast-paced prosecution of the invasion which would allow the United States to decisively beat an army five times its size on the enemy's own terrain.[5] Quick moving regiments of dragoons, mounted riflemen, coupled with the new batteries of "Flying Artillery", allowed American commanders to reposition their forces rapidly and advantageously during the course of the battles. Often quick flanking movements could bring disaster to General Santa Anna's Mexican forces. The idea of moving artillery around extensively, once the battle had begun, reflected a basic change in battle tactics. The newly developed "Flying Artillery" and other light artillery units would, with this method, prove their worth.[6] Reno was assigned the command of a Rocketry and Mountain Howitzer Battery.[7]

Although unique in the American army of Reno's day, war rockets had been around for a long time, having been used as early as the thirteenth century by the Chinese against Mongol attackers. Reno's battery employed two types of rockets, the Congreve and the Hale models. The Congreve rocket had first been adopted by the British army in 1805 and had been employed against the United States in the War of 1812. Indeed, it was Congreve rockets that gave rise to Francis Scott Key's words in "The Star-Spangled Banner": "...the rockets' red glare".[8] The Hale rocket was developed shortly before the Mexican War and was tested by Reno's battery, with the subsequent evaluation that it was not "very perfect".[9]

While rockets had been around for quite a while, the mountain howitzer was fairly new to the American arsenal. It was extremely lightweight, mobile and could be easily disassembled and carried on three horses or mules. When assembled, it could be towed by one horse. Further, it was particularly adaptable to the narrow street fighting in Mexico. Because of its small size and weight, its movement and operation were comparatively simple and, if part of the crew was lost in battle, two artillerists could effectively man it.[10] Yet, despite its smallness, it was rated a twelve-pounder and could effectively fire solid shot against buildings, canister against charging troops, or lob case shot into the midst of the enemy. The mountain howitzer was an excellent weapon for the young officer, Reno. Its mobility may well have been a contributing factor to the later talent Reno showed for flanking movements during the Civil War.

Winfield Scott's invading armada with 12,000 men survived choppy seas to arrive in the harbor of Vera Cruz, Mexico on March 7, 1847. Lieutenant Reno was a part of that military force and would soon get his first taste of combat.[11]

Scott's attack on Mexico was the final part of a four-pronged invasion constituting the United States' strategy for defeating Mexico. General Zachary Taylor initiated the invasion in March 1846, by moving into the Gulf Coast area of Mexico from Fort Brown on the southern tip of Texas. Another army was to attack Chihuahua from El Paso, Texas. A third military force, commanded by Stephen Watts Kearney, was to move west from Fort Leavenworth, Kansas, take Santa Fe, New Mexico, and then drive on and capture California. In the fourth and final thrust, Winfield Scott would depart New Orleans by sea, land at Vera Cruz and deliver the final blow on Mexico City.[12]

As mentioned, Scott's forces arrived at Vera Cruz's harbor on March 7. They did not land, however, until two days later. In most respects that landing was flawless. It started a little before sunset on March 9, with troops of the first division being moved to shore by sixty-seven oared surf boats. The other two divisions followed and the entire army was landed by 10:00 p.m. The New Orleans *Bulletin* of March 27 described the landing:

> The landing of the American army at Vera Cruz has been accomplished in a manner that reflects the highest credit on all concerned, the regularity, precision, and promptness with which it was effected, has probably not been surpassed, if it has been equaled in modern warfare.

> The removal of a large body of troops from numerous transports into boats in an open sea—their subsequent disembarkation on the sea-beach, on an enemy's coast, through the surf, with all their arms and accoutrements without a single error or accident, requires great exertion, skill, and sound judgement. . . . on the present occasion, twelve thousand men were landed in one single day, without, so far as we have heard, the slightest accident or the loss of a single life.[13]

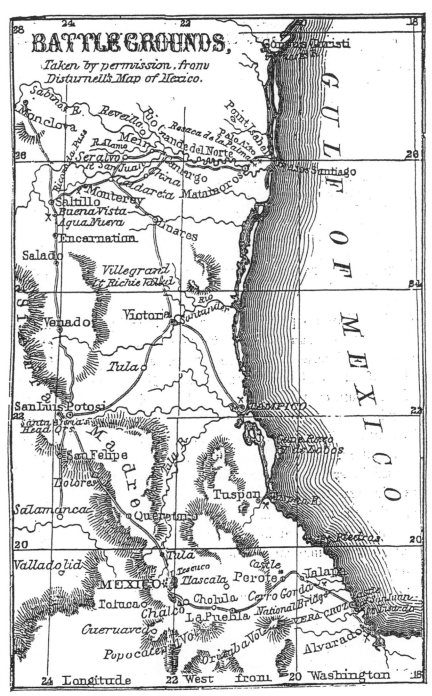

The Mexican War

Some of the artillery was not quite as fortunate as many of the troops. During the first days of the invasion, a strong Gulf wind, known as a "norther", prevented the landing of heavy ordnance. On March 17, there was a lull in the storm and some of the heavy cannons, as well as howitzers, were brought ashore.[14] By that time protective gun emplacements had been dug in strategic positions under the direction of Captain Robert E. Lee. From the relative safety of those emplacements, the artillery launched a vicious bombardment of the city of Vera Cruz and its protective island fortress of San Juan de Ulua. Meanwhile siege lines of five miles length encircled the city.[15]

For all intents, the battle for Vera Cruz was a massive artillery duel between the United States' emplaced cannon and shipboard batteries against 300 Mexican cannon.[16] While the overall siege would last from March 12 to 27, the primary bombardment of the city was from March 23 to 25. Many of the roofs caught fire and a quarter of the city was destroyed. By March 26, the Mexican commander started negotiations to surrender. Final capitulation came the following night. Showing the extent of American artillery fire, it was estimated that a half million pounds of shot and shells had been poured into the city and fortress.[17]

With Vera Cruz in American hands, U.S. forces could now proceed toward Mexico City, but not without impediments. The army of three divisions now totaled only 8,500 men, having been depleted by battle casualties, desertion and considerable sickness. There were few draft animals for the cavalry and artillery, and to carry supplies. Reno's battery crept along slowly in order to conserve the strength of the few animals it had. The Mexicans also would provide additional roadblocks. General Santa Anna, with 12,000 troops, had hurriedly come down from Buena Vista in the north where he had been fighting Zachary Taylor's army.

In his first attempt to block the American army's progress toward the capital, Santa Anna chose an excellent position about 50 miles inland and in the mountains at a commanding elevation known as Cerro Gordo. The route of the U.S. troops followed the National Highway and was channeled through a narrow gap between the base of Cerro Gordo and the Rio de la Plan. With Santa Anna's guns menacing from atop a hill called El Telégrafo, Scott could scarcely attempt a direct frontal assault with his entire army. Rather, he elected to split his forces, initially using elements of Brevet Major General David E. Twiggs' division as a diversionary attack against the Mexican front, while his other two divisions would attempt an attack on the rear and flanking movements on the enemy's left. Twiggs' forces moved out on the morning of April 16 and were essentially successful in their diversionary effort. However, some of his troops were perhaps a bit too aggressive. In chasing Mexicans up the slopes of El Telégrafo, they were pinned down by fire from the top of the hill. Lieutenant Reno's mountain howitzers were rushed to the top of a neighboring hill, Atalaya, to provide the covering fire which would allow the trapped American soldiers to withdraw.[18] If the attack the next day was to have hope of success, however, the American staff realized it was necessary to counter Santa Anna's formidable guns on the hill. During the night, the American 24-pound guns were hoisted by brute manpower up steep slopes to the top of Atalaya. Morning brought the American combined attack of both artillery and infantry.

The Mexican defenders on the hill fought valiantly for a time but finally succumbed to the three-pronged attack. Santa Anna's 2,000 cavalrymen, posted on the National Highway, panicked and bolted. The rout was on. On April 18, 1847, the Battle of Cerro Gordo became another decisive American victory.[19] For his part, Jesse Lee Reno was cited for "Gallant and Meritorious Conduct" and awarded the rank of brevet first lieutenant.

For a time, the road to Mexico City became less hazardous for the small U.S. army, at least from the standpoint of enemy action. The cities of Jalapa, Perote and Puebla were all occupied with little resistance from the opposing army. It was extremely fortunate for Scott that his entry into Puebla in mid-May was unopposed because his forces had diminished to less than 4,500 men and a total of thirteen pieces of artillery.[20] Though the drastic reduction of his army was, in part, the result of the necessity of having to send back home seven regiments of volunteers whose enlistments had run out, a major cause of the depletion of his strength was disease. Prudence dictated that Scott hold up his movement at Puebla until replacements and supplies could be brought inland to him. Among the reenforcements sent him in August were the newly formed (Feb. 1847) Regiment of Voltigeurs and its accompanying six mountain howitzers. His army now was enlarged to 11,000 men.[21] The six mountain howitzers became Reno's Battery, and he joined with the Voltigeurs in what could be considered an excellent pairing of weaponry for the time.[22] The Voltigeurs took their name from elite units originally formed by the French army in 1805 to serve primarily as skirmishers. They were fast-moving and usually had the honor of leading attacks. As skirmishers, they did not fight in close ranks. During the Mexican War the Voltigeurs fought as irregular riflemen performing such duties as clearing woods. They were disbanded near the end of the war.[23]

Reenforced, the Americans moved out of Puebla on August 7, 1847, only to be challenged once again by Santa Anna at Contreras. In the confrontation there, on August 19 and 20, Reno's battery joined with two other artillery units in an attempt to soften Mexican defenses.[24] In the subsequent fighting the greatly outnumbered Americans again surprised and outflanked the well entrenched Mexicans. The main attack by the Americans lasted only 17 minutes, but it thoroughly overwhelmed Santa Anna's men sending them fleeing in total panic.

Scott gave the order to pursue the enemy but, surprisingly, the Mexicans were able to make another and much more effective stand at Churubusco. There a large convent had been turned into a fortress. Repeated charges by the Americans were driven back initially. The artillery of both sides, including Reno's Battery, played a significant role in the Battle of Churubusco. Strongly contested, the Americans suffered more than a thousand casualties. Finally, however, they wore the defenders down and could again claim victory. Only one more roadblock stood in the way of capturing Mexico City and winning the war—the Castle of Chapultepec.

Both opponents took a two week respite to regroup before the final American assault. Scott's force, now only 8,300, faced a Mexican army of nearly 20,000. Further complicating his task was the fact that the Mexican capital was protected by the large and formidable Castle of Chapultepec, located on a bluff about 150 feet high. Scott implaced his artillery for a bombardment of the fortress on the evening of September 11 and commenced firing the next morning at daybreak. The artillery duel continued until eight o'clock on the morning of September 13 when the American guns fell silent. This signalled the beginning of the infantry assault on the castle. In this attack, Reno's mountain howitzers supported four companies of Voltigeurs and two infantry regiments.[25] Valiant fighters though they were, the Mexican defenders were forced to give up Chapultepec on September 13, 1847. With Chapultepec taken, the final assault on the city proper was made. At one point in the street fighting, with Mexican snipers on rooftops, it was reported that army Lieutenant U.S. Grant and navy Lieutenant Rafael Semmes engineered the raising of two mountain howitzers to church steeples where they could rain down fire on Mexican defenders.[26] It is not recorded whether or not the guns were from Reno's Battery, but such was a possibility.

Reno, for his action at Chapultepec, would again be cited for "Gallant and Meritorious conduct" and would be made a brevet captain. He also received a wound at that battle, but the nature and severity of it were not specified in his records. Likely it was not severe, otherwise General Scott would have made mention of it, as he did in other cases in his official report of September 18, 1847.[27] However, in that report the commanding general twice cited the 24-year-old lieutenant for his outstanding service. In regard to the battle for Mexico City he wrote: "The mountain howitzer battery, under Lieutenant Reno, of the ordnance, deserves, also, to be particularly mentioned. Attached to the Voltigeurs, it followed the movements of that regiment, and again won applause."[28] And again near the end of his report, Scott said: "The ordnance officers, Captain Huger, Lieutenants Hagner, Stone and Reno, were highly effective, and distinguished at the several batteries."[29]

4— PEACETIME IN THE REGULAR ARMY

The victorious army began its return home from Mexico in June, 1848.[1] Reno literally returned home, for he was assigned "Special Duty" at Erie, Pennsylvania, where his family had moved. The special duty assignment most likely was in the form of military leave.

With the war over, Reno reverted to his regular rank of second lieutenant. On the army rolls, this was for the purposes of seniority and pay. He would, however, be permitted to continue to use his brevet title of "Captain". The confusing Army custom of bestowing brevet ranks on officers began in 1806. Essentially, they were honorary ranks awarded for meritorious conduct but, in certain cases, to the confusion of the system, they actually could be recognized as real rank.[2] This was a situation in which Reno found himself at a later time. Suffice it to say that he was never known by any other title than "Captain" until promoted to brigadier general in 1861.

For the next five years Reno drew a variety of odd jobs, and one might wonder why he stayed in the Army when so many other West Point graduates were leaving the service for more lucrative fields. Indeed, though more than 1,300 men had graduated from the academy, only about 600 had remained in the army by 1847.[3] The fact that he drew assignments at what were then choice locations, rather than being buried, as it were, in some remote western post, may have had something to do with his decision to remain in the army.

Reno's first post-war duty was as assistant professor of mathematics at his alma mater from January 9, 1849 until July 16 of that year. That fall he was designated the secretary of a board assigned to prepare a manual for a "System of Instruction for Heavy Artillery." This task occupied his time until mid-October of 1850. Surely, both these assignments must have seemed rather bland to Reno after the excitement of Mexico. However, a new form of excitement was in store for him at his next duty station.

For the better part of the next three years, Reno served as assistant to the Ordnance Board in Washington, D.C. This choice plum of an assignment, at the fountainhead of the Ordnance Corps might seem good fortune enough, but Reno was to get an even greater benefit from the Washington assignment—love! Likely, it was during this three-year tour of duty in the nation's capital that Jesse Reno fell in love with the charming and well educated Mary Bradley Beanes Cross. She was born on December 7, 1828 and was five years younger than he. That they would meet was not unexpected, for Mary came from a prominent Washington military family and would doubtless have traveled in social circles that would have brought her in contact with the handsome young hero of the Mexican War.

Mary's father, Colonel Trueman Cross, was Zachary Taylor's assistant quartermaster general in 1846. On April 10, shortly before the beginning of hostilities with Mexico, Colonel Cross rode out of Fort Brown, Texas, to scout the area. While away from the safety of the American encampment, he was intercepted and thought to have been killed by a band of Mexican bandits under the leadership of "Falcon".[4] Though not a combat death, Colonel Cross's murder was a factor in causing American settlers in the Southwest and California to rebel against the Mexican government and to seek admission into the United States. Thus, in a sense, his death was significant in the achieving of America's "Manifest Destiny". On November 21, 1845, Colonel Cross had written a letter to Washington detailing the fact that the army had no means of field transportation whatever.[5] When he was brought back to the nation's capital for burial, his funeral cortege included President James K. Polk, other high government officials and ranking officers of all the military services.[6]

Mary Cross's mother, the lovely Eliza Bradley Beanes Cross, was the daughter of a famous Maryland doctor, William Bradley Beanes. In 1814, about fourteen years before his death, the elderly physician had been temporarily held prisoner with Francis Scott Key aboard the British ship *Surprise* near Baltimore. Inspired by the event and the doctor's questions, Key wrote the "Star Spangled Banner" which he later dedicated to Beanes.[7] Among the many coincidences of Reno's life was the fact that Dr. Beanes had lived near the mouth of the Patuxent River and the ship which transported Reno and his troops to North Carolina during the Civil War was the *Patuxent*.

After nearly seven years of active military service, Jesse Reno finally achieved the seniority necessary to be promoted to the rank of first lieutenant on March 3, 1853. Whether this elevated status was the cause of Jesse's reassignment or whether, out of boredom, he may have requested it, is not known. In either case, Reno was loaned by the Ordnance Department to the Corps of Topographical Engineers for a special assignment. His orders directed him to conduct a survey for a new military road to run from the mouth of the Big Sioux River to Mendota, Minnesota.[8] Any wedding plans Reno and Mary Cross may have had would be delayed for a few months.

The mass migration of settlers to areas west of the Mississippi River in the mid-nineteenth century brought with it a great need for lines of communication and commerce, as well as routes that could facilitate the military protection of those settlers. Minnesota, like many of the newly developing territories and states, lacked the funds to generate a much-needed transportation system. Through the efforts of Henry Hastings Sibley, Minnesota's first delegate to the United States House of Representatives, a bill was passed on July 8, 1850, granting Minnesota federal funds to build four roads and survey a fifth one. The latter route was designated to connect the two main rivers in the area, the Mississippi and the Missouri. Specifically, it would run from the mouth of the Big Sioux River in Iowa to Mendota, Minnesota. On present day maps, this would be from Sioux City to Minneapolis.[9] The task of laying out this route was given to Jesse Reno.

On May 5, 1853, Reno received his orders to proceed with the road survey project. He departed Washington with his assistant, a civil engineer named James Tilton. Tilton was the only engineer assigned to Reno's expedition. The two men first went to St. Louis, Missouri where they took on supplies. While there Reno also employed a crew of 16 men for the project, including a surveyor named Cross. From St. Louis, the party booked passage on the steamer *El Paso* for Council Bluffs, Iowa. After procuring horses and oxen at Council Bluffs and nearby Weston, Lieutenant Reno and his group started their 120-mile march along the Missouri to the mouth of the Big Sioux. Reno described this phase of the journey in his report:

We followed the road to Fort Pierre, on the left bank of the river, meeting with little difficulty, except at the crossing of the Little Sioux, where we were two days in passing over six miles of overflowed bottoms, or wet prairie, extending from the bluffs to the river. Here the oxen mired, and we had to transport the baggage, provisions, and instruments, by hand, and by the same means to drag the empty wagons. However, in dry weather this route offers no obstacle to teams, all the streams being bridged, or having ferries over them.

The bottoms along the Missouri are from five to fifteen miles broad, in rich alluvial soil, with occasional pretty groves of cottonwood and oak, which relieve otherwise monotonous scenery. There are as yet very few settlers in this region, but, as the grass is very fine, it will before long be in great demand for raising cattle for the California and Oregon emigrants—a very lucrative business, and rapidly increasing in importance.[10]

As they neared the end of the first leg of the trip, Reno's party suffered the worst calamity of the entire expedition. Camping along Floyd's Creek, on 15 June, one of the young men, Cyrus Scott of Kentucky, was bathing in the creek and ventured into deep water. Not being able to swim, he perished before anyone in the group could come to his aid. Reno wrote of Scott: " . . . by his amiability and many good qualities, gained the good opinion of all."[11]

The survey party reached the vicinity of the mouth of the Big Sioux on June 17 and there they found a small settlement made up for the most part of French voyageurs and their Indian wives. The Frenchmen, having tired of working for the American Fur Company, had sought a more sedentary life, and cultivated a few acres of corn and potatoes to supplement their diet of fish and game. Prophetically, however, Lt. Reno noted the following in his report:

> But a new era is about to dawn. The restless and enterprising Anglo-Saxon has, within the last year, set his foot here and laid out a town—a certain indication that the region has passed forever from the Indian and his mercurial friend, the voyageur.[12]

The Reno party made their camp on the farm of one Bruyere, a French-Canadian who had lived in the area for twenty years. Bruyere was married to a Sioux and was reported to have "a most beneficial influence over all the Indians in the vicinity." Reno had hoped to talk with Bruyere and perhaps gain valuable information about a suitable route for the road, since the Frenchman was one of only a few white men who had made the trip from the Missouri to the mouth of the Minnesota River. Unfortunately, Bruyere was not at home at the time, and Reno had to proceed without the benefit of his knowledge.[13]

Unable to obtain a white guide to accompany them, Reno hired an Indian who claimed to know the area well. This, however, proved unsatisfactory, for the self-professed guide left them unannounced after only three days on the trail. Reno indicated that they probably suffered no great loss by the Indian's departure: "He was of little assistance, however, having a very inadequate idea of the kind of country best suited for a good road, and not at all disposed to comprehend the instructions of the engineer to avoid the hills—his idea of a good road being the shortest distance betweeen two points that could be passed over on horseback."[14]

After spending three days exploring the area around the mouth of the Big Sioux, the Reno party began their road-surveying trip on June 20, 1853. The route laid out would ultimately be 279 miles in length and would take them about 2 1/2 months to survey. To relate Reno's route to present-day maps and locations, it started near Sioux City, Iowa, cut diagonally across northwest Iowa, crossing into Minnesota about ten miles northeast of Esterville, Iowa, on to Mankato and thence to the Minneapolis-St. Paul area.[15]

In addition to describing the features of the terrain as they related to the proposed roadway, Reno proved to be a keen and sensitive observer of other natural surroundings. Throughout the journey he recorded detailed physical descriptions of lakes, woods, marshes, prairies and streams as well as the settlements, villages and existing roads. He seemed most impressed by: "The healthfulness of the climate and the productiveness of the soil in Minnesota [which] are not surpassed by the most favored regions of our country."[16]

To simplify the surveying process, Reno elected to break down the road route into six divisions, each being about 40 to 50 miles in length. He also made individual road construction cost estimates for each of the six divisions, based on its terrain. Although the crew had an odometer for measuring distances, Reno determined it to be unsuitable because its use took more time than measuring with a 100-foot chain. Thus, using the chain, the crew marked the route with a stake every 600 feet along the way. In his report, Reno also noted that his surveyor, Cross, took great care in making his observations. As they progressed along the route, they prepared a map and sketched the terrain.

The first 100 miles or so across the Iowa prairie offered no great excitement for the band of surveyors. One morning, however, while camped along a stream called Ocheyedan, the monotony was broken by the approach of a small herd of buffalo. "After an exciting chase", Reno reported, "we succeeded in cutting off and pistoling one with our Colt's revolvers; and bearing him into camp, he proved a most welcome addition to our commissariat." After reaching Minnesota, Reno twice commented as to how tasty the fish in the lakes and streams were.[17]

After travelling for about 180 miles through prairie, unoccupied by white men, Lt. Reno and his band were joyful on reaching Mankato. There, in south central Minnesota, was an already flourishing settlement of "200 intelligent and energetic countrymen." Reno further described Mankato as being in the heart of a rich agricultural region which possessed all the elements of future prosperity and importance. While continuing on to their destination at Mendota, Jesse made glowing reports of the many beautiful lakes and the bountiful forests. Also, he employed his prerogative as the ranking officer to name certain places along the route. These included Lake Mary, for his wife-to-be, Lake Tilton, for his engineer and Lake Cross, probably for his surveyor, though possibly also for Mary Cross.[18]

On September 7, 1853, the *Minnesota Democrat* of St. Paul, reported that Captain Reno and his surveying party had arrived at that city a few days earlier. For Reno, the field work for the survey was completed and he would return to Washington to compile his report. Over all, he figured that the cost of constructing the road would be $52,475.68, or an average of $188.18 per mile. In support of his assistant, he recommended that James Tilton superintend the road construction, should Congress make the necessary appropriation. Further, he recommended that should sufficient funds not be made available for building the entire road, at least the Mankato to Mendota portion should be constructed. As it later turned out, between 1856 and 1858, this portion of the road would be the only part ever to be built.[19]

In closing his report, Reno waxed poetic:

It is needless to enlarge upon the importance of establishing a road through this region; its increasing importance is too well known to require any additional arguments in its favor. The 20,000 inhabitants of the best classes of our hardy pioneers and enterprising farmers now scattered over its broad extent, and busily employed in making solitudes— hitherto untrodden save by the savage—smile with beautiful villages, and the earth teem with abundant fruits, will not ask in vain the fostering hand of government.[20]

With field work completed in Iowa and Minnesota, Reno returned to Washington in the fall of 1853 to commence the laborious task of collating all of the road survey data and compile his report. Since the report would be submitted to Secretary of War Jefferson Davis, and then on to Congress, the young lieutenant doubtless faced the usual bureaucratic roadblocks and other delays. More than a half year passed before he was able to submit his final report.

However, Reno had other thoughts on his mind. Now back near his beloved Mary, they could make wedding plans. On November 1, 1853, Jesse and Mary exchanged vows before Rector Smith Pyne at

St. John's Episcopal Church in Washington, D.C.[21] St. John's apparently was Mary's regular church, for in later days she makes mention of attending it several times.

Following the wedding, Reno continued working on his report until its submission on April 1, 1854, to the chief of the Corps of Topographical Engineers, Colonel John J. Abert. Abert approved it and forwarded it to Jefferson Davis on April 24 and Davis sent it to the House of Representatives the next day. It would seem that Reno's work was well done, for the 33rd Congress ordered, on April 28, that it be printed as House Executive Document No. 97. With the approval of his report, Reno was relieved of any further responsibility on the project. From April 25 to July 15 that summer he was assigned "Coast Survey" duty, the specific nature of which is not noted.

After eight years of service as an officer of the Ordnance Corps, Reno was finally posted to a position truly in keeping with his title. This was as assistant ordnance officer at the Frankford Arsenal in northeast Philadelphia. In many respects this was likely the most pleasant and longest period together in Jesse and Mary's brief married life. The Frankford Arsenal was the type of post that would be referred to, in modern military parlance, as a "country club" assignment. It was the second oldest of the U.S. arsenals, dating from 1816. It had been considerably enlarged in 1837 and 1849, so that by the time of the Reno's arrival there, it was a well-developed army establishment. Lying along the juncture of Frankford Creek and the Delaware River, the arsenal had many beautiful large shade trees bordering a spacious parade ground and sheltering comfortable officers' quarters.

In many ways Frankford would be an idyllic time in the lives of the young couple. They started their family first with a son, Lewis, followed by a daughter, Marian. Their greatest misfortune at Frankford, however, was the loss of little Marian when she was only six months old. Fortunately, for their happiness then, was the fact that they could not know that little Lewis would also die after eight years. For the most part, however, this was a time of the "good life" for Mary and Jesse. They had both a cow and servants, the latter including the nanny, Biddy, who stayed with Mary for some time. They also had a houseman named King. About the only major discomfort of the area was the profusion of mosquitos rising from the nearby wetlands. Mary once wrote that little Lewis was badly bitten by them, despite sleeping under a net.[22]

Reno also was fortunate in having a compatible commanding officer. Brevet Major Peter V. Hagner and his wife, Sue, proved to be lasting friends of the Renos. They also had little boys with whom

Lewis could play. Major Hagner had graduated from West Point ten years before Reno. Both were ordnance officers who served under General Scott in Mexico. They likely became acquainted during that time. After Reno completed his tour of duty at Frankford and was assigned to Albert Sidney Johnston's western expedition, the Hagners continued to watch over Mary and her little family.[23] Four years later, Reno relieved Peter Hagner as commander of the arsenal at Ft. Leavenworth. During the Civil War, Hagner continued as an ordnance officer, rising to the rank of lieutenant colonel.

5— WHEN THE SAINTS WENT MARCHING

A desire for religious independence and the actions of two strong-willed men, President James Buchanan and Mormon leader Brigham Young, decided Reno's next military assignment. Ever since the 1846 settlement of the Church of Jesus Christ of Latter Day Saints in the Great Salt Lake area of Utah, there had been growing tension between the church leadership and federal authorities. The Mormons, for their part, desired to be governed by only members of their own faith and disdained the intrusion of "gentile" settlers. The federal government, on the other hand, objected to the independent stand of the Mormon leadership and especially to the church's condoning of polygamy. Utah had achieved territorial status in 1850 but had been turned down several times by Congress for statehood, largely because of the polygamy issue. Suspicions grew on both sides, and by the summer of 1857, President Buchanan feared a revolt by the Mormons. Further, he felt that only a display of force could bring order to Utah.[1] Accordingly, in May, 1857, and perhaps somewhat unnecessarily, he ordered the assembling of an army of 2,500 at Fort Leavenworth, Kansas, to march west and quell any uprising by the Saints.[2] A force of this size had to be fully staffed, including a chief of ordnance. Colonel Henry K. Craig, commanding the Ordnance Corps, chose Jesse Lee Reno for the task.

Although he had been previously advised of the assignment, Reno did not receive orders relieving him of duty at Frankford Arsenal until June 25, 1857. Also at that time Col. Craig provided specific instructions concerning the method of accumulating ordnance supplies for the Utah expedition, personnel requirements, and the route to be followed to Fort Leavenworth.[3] Pursuant to these orders, Reno enlisted 12 men for the military venture, promising to discharge them in 12 to 15 months.[4] As with almost all such groups, he would get both good and bad men. Directly supervising his little detachment was family friend, John N. Kalapaza. Reno had Kalapaza appointed master armorer before the departure. Later, in letters to Mary, he reflected on his great satisfaction with the choice. As in the case of his assistant during the Minnesota road survey, Captain Reno again displayed his support of productive subordinates. While in the West, Reno requested that Col. Craig seek an officer's commission for Kalapaza.[5] Shortly after Reno's departure from Frankford Arsenal, Major Hagner wrote to him advising that one of his enlistees, William Price Major, had made false statements at his enlistment. According to a woman claiming to be Major's wife, he had stated that he was a blacksmith when, in fact, he had been a clerk in a dry goods store. The woman, described as "seven months gone", cried bitterly that Reno had taken her husband off and left her penniless.[6] Apparently, Major took advantage of an opportunity to skip out on his wife and to draw better pay in the process. If in truth he had been a blacksmith, he would have drawn pay similar to a sergeant, rather than a private's meager stipend.

On Saturday evening, June 27, Reno waved goodbye from his carriage to his wife and young son, Lewis. Both Jesse and Mary anticipated the Utah assignment would keep them apart for only about a year. In reality, his western tour of duty would last for two years. Following Col. Craig's orders, Reno proceeded first to Allegheny Arsenal at Pittsburgh, Pennsylvania, to requisition necessary ordnance stores there. Kalapaza and the other enlisted men were sent to pack stores at St. Louis Arsenal, and there to wait for Reno. En route, Reno's trunk was lost and he made claim for $300 restitution for its contents. In a subsequent letter to him, Mary joked about his exorbitant claim, stating that she could not see where it could possibly be worth more than $200.[7]

After acquiring such ordnance supplies as he felt needed for the expedition from the Frankford, Allegheny and St. Louis arsenals, Reno and his little band proceeded on to assemble at Fort Leavenworth, Kansas. There they reported to the commanding officer for further instructions. As with many hastily formed military expeditions, the activities at Fort Leavenworth were in a state of bedlam. Troops were being brought in from Florida, Minnesota and elsewhere. Some of these were well-trained regulars, while others were raw recruits. Many of the men arriving at the fort were also in poor health, due to scurvy and other ailments acquired enroute.[8]

General confusion and poor planning also contributed to the delay in departing for Utah. Although the government had formulated its plan for putting down the supposed Mormon rebellion in late May, seven weeks transpired before the vanguard of troops moved out of Fort Leavenworth. This and other complications along the route would thrust the expedition against the hazards of the oncoming winter.[9]

Even before departure, two serious problems arose to hinder the success of the expedition. The commander, Brigadier General William S. Harney, and the Second Dragoon Regiment were both diverted from the Utah expedition and put at the disposal of Governor Robert J. Walker of Kansas. A political crisis had arisen which led Walker to believe that he needed both Harney and the Second Dragoons to maintain peace in his territory.[10] The loss of Harney from the Utah expedition, for a time, deprived the venture of adequate leadership. The command of the initial convoy fell to the leader of the Tenth Infantry Regiment, Colonel E. B. Alexander. This officer, by his vacillations and indecision, would prove to be inadequate for the task ahead of him.[11] The loss of the Second Dragoons until mid-September deprived the long and strung-out caravan of its primary defensive force, since the dragoons were to serve as its cavalry escort. Without them, the expedition would be subjected to the depredations of both Mormons and Indians.

While at Leavenworth, Reno also had his frustrations. In addition to his demanding job as chief of ordnance, he was given command of one of the expedition's two artillery units, Battery C of the Third Artillery. It would be nearly a year before he was relieved of the additional task.[12] The other battery of artillery was commanded by Captain John W. Phelps. Like Jesse Reno, Phelps had been an artillery officer in the War with Mexico and would later be a Union general in the Civil War. Phelps was a strong abolitionist from Vermont who eventually resigned his commission from the Union army because his action of recruiting black soldiers was not backed by the administration. He became the anti-Mason candidate for president in 1880.[13]

Finally, on July 18, the first detachments of troops departed from Fort Leavenworth. The lead-off group, the 10th Infantry Regiment, was accompanied by Phelps' battery. Jesse Reno's artillery followed with the 5th Infantry Regiment. These initial groups were made up of about 1,200 men.[14] Interspersed in the long convoy were supply trains including over 400 mule-drawn wagons and two thousand head of beef cattle.[15] The route to be followed west was one familiar to pioneers heading for Utah, Oregon and California. The convoy of troops, cannons and supply trains extended over more than seven miles of the dusty and unexciting trail. On occasion, perhaps to relieve his boredom, Jesse Reno drew sketches to send to his young son, Lewis. Mary wrote of Lewis's appreciation of the pictures but, unfortunately, never described them. One can but guess what the loving father drew to enchant his toddler son—perhaps a buffalo or a jack rabbit on the western prairie.

After leaving Fort Leavenworth, the expedition moved west to the Big Blue River, then north to intercept the slow-moving Platte. The westward movement to the dreary camp at Fort Kearny posed no real problems for the strung out and virtually indefensible convoy. Water and forage were available for the animals, and usually the troops could cover 15 to 20 miles in a day's march. The relatively easy march ceased after passing Fort Kearny. Barely out of sight of the fort, just 20 miles to the west, Cheyenne Indians attacked the convoy, drove off 800 head of cattle and killed one driver.[16] Much of this disaster could be credited to the poor planning of the commander, Col. Alexander, who lacking the services of the dragoon regiment as a mobile defensive force, also placed some of the supply trains in the convoy miles away from military units, leaving them indefensible. Reno wrote to his wife, Mary, of this fiasco. She wrote back that, while she was disturbed by the "frolic" of the Indians, she ought to content herself "that they chose the cattle" instead of the men.[17]

Continuing west along the Platte, Colonel Alexander and his command arrived at Fort Laramie on September 1. Up to this point, other than the incursions of the Indians, no disaster had befallen President Buchanan's intrepid warriors. Though still unofficial, good news arrived to inform the troops that a new commander, Colonel Albert Sidney Johnston, would soon be taking over the Utah expedition. In actuality, Johnston had been given command of the expedition on August 29, 1857.[18] Unfortunately for the troops involved, it took Johnston two months to catch up with them. In the meantime, they had to live under Alexander's dubious leadership. From Fort Laramie west, there would be a new harasser, in addition to the Indians, to impede the progress of the army. This was in the form of Mormons striking the convoy wherever and whenever they could. Mother Nature joined also to add roadblocks to the troop movement. To make matters worse, winter was coming, and it would be record setting. The oncoming cold weather, coupled with the Mormons burning grasslands, left little forage for the thousands of animals accompanying the convoy. Before reaching winter quarters at Fort Bridger, Reno lost half of the livestock supporting his artillery battery.[19] The vacillation and indecision of Colonel Alexander continued to hinder the progress of the army and it was becoming apparent that they could not reach Salt Lake City before the winter snows blocked their way. Alexander's troops finally reached Ham's Fork on the Green River, 35 miles east of Fort Bridger, at the end of September. Here he established Camp Winfield. Unfortunately, he wasted the month of October in an abortive effort to reach Utah by way of the Bear River. Retracing their route back to Ham's Fork, Alexander and his army reestablished themselves at Camp Winfield.[20]

On November 4, Col. Johnston arrived at Camp Winfield to take over command from Alexander. This did much to improve the spirits of the cold, disorganized and demoralized troops. After assaying the situation and realizing that their position at Camp Winfield was untenable, Colonel Johnston on November 6, ordered the troops to advance on Fort Bridger, then held by the Mormons. Travelling through storms of snow and sleet, with the temperature at times reaching 16 degrees below zero, the convoy took 15 days to cover the 35 miles. Dead horses and cattle, killed by hunger and the extreme cold, marked the entire route from Camp Winfield to Fort Bridger. The Mormons, forewarned of the advance, fell back to their fortifications in Echo Canyon, about halfway between Fort Bridger and Salt Lake City. Before departing, however, they burned all buildings at Fort Bridger, leaving only the stone walls of the main building standing.[21]

Using the remains of Fort Bridger as the anchor for the northeast end of his encampment, Johnston stationed his units along two miles or so of Black's Fork. He named the entire settlement Camp Scott, and it was to be home for the Utah expeditionary forces for the next seven months. Johnston also had the stone enclosure fortified by placing cannon in the southwest and northeast corners, and by constructing earthworks and a moat. Protected by two companies of troops, the unroofed structure served as a storehouse for some of the supplies. As the ordnance officer, Captain Reno stored ammunition and other ordnance items within the 6-foot thick walls of the fort, using tarpaulins and rawhides to protect them from the weather. He noted that these coverings offered no protection from fire, however. He also reported that Colonel Johnston deemed it impractical to build a magazine that winter.[22]

With the harsh winter and with food and clothing in short supply for his men, Reno was further encumbered by still having to command an artillery battery in addition to supervising all ordnance activities. Colonel Craig, chief of ordnance in Washington, was particularly irate about the fact that Reno was saddled with the artillery duties. He wrote a three-page letter to Secretary of War John B. Floyd, expressing his displeasure and requesting that the Secretary use his position to relieve Reno of this second job. Moreover, Craig was upset that Reno had been directed by Col. Johnston to assign his ordnance men to serve with the artillery battery. Whether or not Floyd interceded in behalf of Jesse Reno is not known. It was well into the following summer before Reno was able to shake the responsibility of commanding the cannon battery.[23]

Although supplies were scarce and the weather cold, the army fared relatively well under the circumstances. That the morale and health of the troops were maintained as well as they were, should largely be credited to Johnston's outstanding leadership. Ironically, the blundering Colonel Alexander can be considered the hero of the entire campaign. Had Alexander been a more effective leader, the army would probably have reached Utah by the fall of 1857, during a time when both the federal government and the Mormons were ready to do battle. Alexander's delays and the harsh winter provided the time necessary for cooler heads to prevail. Both Brigham Young and President Buchanan had the long winter to consider the rashness of their original plans. By June of 1858, peace emissaries had worked out a face-saving arrangement whereby the army would be permitted to maintain an occupation force in Utah, but well out of the way of most of the Saints.[24] The potential civil war in Utah was averted, thus saving thousands of lives. Safe also were the cities and settlements which might have been lost as result of the Mormon scorched earth plan.

In the meantime and throughout the winter, Reno and his ordnance men were active in repairing weapons and outfitting several units with necessary arms. Working in conjunction with Colonel Johnston, he also requisitioned arms and munitions which they anticipated would be needed for the campaign in the spring.[25] It should be noted that, in April, Reno was directed to provide to Mr. C. Drexler, "Collector of Specimens of Natural History, for the Smithsonian Institute [sic, Institution]", five pounds of shot, powder and percussion caps.[26]

With occupation agreements reached and his army resupplied, Albert Sidney Johnston was ready to begin his march to Salt Lake City on June 13, 1858. Under the terms reached by the negotiating parties, Johnston's army was permitted to march to Salt Lake City, and with a show of force, go through it. However, his troops were not to stop anywhere within the city. If they defied that provision of the agreements, the Saints had vowed to torch Salt Lake City. In light of this, all Mormons had evacuated the town, except those left behind to verify that the army abided by the strict letter of the agreed terms. Accordingly, on June 26, the mighty military force of the United States marched into the near-deserted city with bands playing and little else to detract from the rumbling sounds of marching feet. The unheralded and certainly unapplauded Federal parade moved through the deserted city along South Temple Street and westward without stopping. Reno's battery of artillery was positioned near the middle of the long column.[27]

Holding to the treaty terms, Johnston kept his troops moving straight through the city and on to the agreed upon encampment site in Cedar Valley, 36 miles south of Salt Lake City. There he created the largest military installation in the United States at that time, which he named Camp Floyd after the secretary of war. Here Reno supervised the construction of the large post arsenal. While many of the buildings were made of adobe, Reno's arsenal, with its three-foot thick walls, was constructed of stone quarried from the Oquirrh Mountains.[28]

With the erection of the large military post came the usual migration of profit-seekers. Dance halls, saloons and gambling establishments rapidly arose, and soon the adjoining community of Fairfield became the third largest town in Utah Territory. Numerous activities were available to provide release for the soldiers from the boring routine of the military camp.[29] To what extent Captain Reno's troops partook of these various amusements is not known, but likely much of their time, as well as pay, was spent in Fairfield.

Doubtless a welcome change for Reno was finally his relief of command of Battery C of the 3rd Artillery. Brevet Major John F. Reynolds assumed command of the unit in the fall of 1858. Reynolds would achieve, as did Jesse Reno, high rank during the Civil War and, as with Reno, lose his life early in that war.[30]

Routine ordnance duties occupied much of Reno's time. These responsibilities included the maintenance and storage of large amounts of ammunition and weapons. Additionally, he was in charge of issuing such supplies to the forces at Camp Floyd. On October 30, 1858, Johnston, now a brigadier general, directed that Captain Reno sell guns to those quartermaster men then being discharged and going to California and in need of weapons.[31]

Incomplete post returns from Camp Floyd for the period do not reflect it, but we can only surmise that Jesse Reno returned on leave to Washington, D.C. to visit his beloved family around the end of March, 1859. This is indicated by the fact that Mary gave birth to their fourth child, Conrad, on December 28, 1859. The visit brought only brief joy to Mary, however. Their baby son, Alexander, who had been born in February, died in May. Perhaps easing her sorrow from the loss of little Alexander, was Reno's return to her near the end of June, 1858.[32]

Starting on the day after Reno's departure from Frankford Arsenal for Utah Territory, his wife Mary wrote letters to him each

week, usually on Sundays. For reasons unknown, a few of her letters ultimately found their way to a military file in the National
Archives.[33] Of Mary's ten letters stored there, all but one were written at a time when Reno was en route to Utah. Thus, it seems prob-
able that these letters may have been lost for a time, never reached
Reno, and finally came to rest in a file of military correspondence
under his name. Whatever may have been the cause of their unusual
storage, we should be thankful for the insight they provide us into
the lives of Jesse and Mary.

Although the professional side of Reno's life is fairly well docu-
mented, information concerning his private life is meager indeed.
Long after his death, a daughter-in-law accumulated many of the
Reno family records.[34] Unfortunately, these appear to have been discarded or lost, and extensive efforts have failed to recover them. A
lack of a continuing line of descendants has further complicated
the acquisition of material that might give additional insight into
Reno's personality and character. His youngest son and last surviving descendent died in 1947. Though the two youngest of Jesse
Reno's sons were married for many years, there were no grandchildren to carry on his lineage.

From written accounts of Reno's military achievements, we can
draw some conclusions. We know that he was short, five foot five
inches in height, had a rather stocky build, smoked cigars, could
certainly be firm in action and, if the occasion arose, could lose his
temper. We know too that he was a brilliant military strategist and
an especially talented leader. Though some have erroneously implied an insensitivity on his part, he was, rather, the kind of military
leader who took no nonsense when plying his trade in battle. At that
unfortunate time in our history when many militarily unskilled and
blundering leaders would cause the deaths of so many young men,
Reno was among the few talented and successful generals who, with
firm determination won battles and gained the deep respect of his
subordinates. But, what of the man Reno, the husband, the father—
what was he really like? For this view into his personality, we must
utilize the writings of his loving wife, Mary.

Although Mary's letters provide an almost singular source for
insight into the private aspects of Reno's character, one cannot but
feel being an intruder when reading them. It is especially painful for
the reader to know that many of the aspirations expressed by the
young wife would never be realized.

Mary's letters not only reflect her excellent education and distinct intelligence, but in addition, her charm and ability to cope with
situations that, in her time would have normally been accomplished
by the man of the house. Throughout her writing one can also readily

observe that her love for Jesse was surely deep and abiding. As with so many wives of career military men, Mary faced, and resolved, many problems that arose after her husband's sudden and probably unexpected departure. She did this despite the fact that she was from a prominent family and accustomed to the help of servants. From selling family property to arranging for the moving of furniture and securing a new residence, Mary displayed the competence that is often hidden in soldiers' wives until that time arises when they are suddenly called upon to fend for themselves. Her activities, as she describes them in her letters of the 1850s, could easily fit into a modern-day military wife's letters.

Although we lack pictures of Mary, we can speculate about her appearance. If the paintings of her beautiful mother and handsome and distinguished-looking father can be any guide, she must have been attractive. Mary, herself, may have given us a clue as to why we now do not find any pictures of her. In writing to Jesse Reno before she left Frankford Arsenal, she mentioned that she had gone to the city of Philadelphia with friends, and while there, attempted to pick up "my dear little daguerreotype which I had so fixed my heart upon." From her account, her picture, along with several others, had been stolen from the shop a week earlier. Mary failed to tell us why the picture was in the shop, but possibly it was for tinting, a common practice at the time. Perhaps accounting for the dearth of pictures of Mary is her further statement: "...I shall probably never meet again with a likeness that would satisfy me as well." This unfortunate loss was ours as well as hers.

In her initial letter to Reno, written the day after his departure, Mary gives us an insight into Reno the husband, the master of the household, friend and father. She wrote: "The servants seemed much distressed at your departure and I heard a good many sobs and groans after you left. I surely believe everyone loves you"; and further, "Mrs. Hagner sends her love to you... and says the place seems deserted already." In closing that first letter, Mary adds: "Good night my darling husband May God bless you. This is my prayer for you day and night and little Lewis uttered it before his nap of his own accord, and carried your daguerreotype to his pillow."

Mary's will and determination were challenged almost as soon as her husband had left for Utah. Before departing, Reno had sold the family milk cow to a man named McCairn with the provision that Mary might keep it for "several days" after July 1, should she stay on briefly at Frankford Arsenal. Despite this agreement, McCairn showed up to take the cow on June 29. Mary described him as a little tipsy and said: "We had an up and down talk and he finally consented to the cow's remaining as long as I wished. I fixed upon the 6th as coming, I thought, within the terms of the bargain, but made him to understand that I received it as a right - not as a favor from him which he was inclined to make it."

One cannot help being entranced by the writing of this confident and capable woman. Mary's letters were full of news about family and friends but never mentioned any problems that might alarm or upset her husband. She showed her deep love for Jesse by admonishing him to take care of himself, in order that he might safely come back to her.

Through Mary's letters we also learn that she lived in Washington, D.C. with her brother William during much of Reno's time in Utah. William, with another brother, Alex, was trying to buy a plantation from a Mr. Dexter of Boston. This appears to have been an intra-family business transaction, with Mary perhaps having a financial interest. William also owned a slave woman named Agnes of whom Mary wrote: "Brother William has almost made up his mind to sell Agnes. She is really unbearable, and has got now to wearing everybody's nicest clothes." Mary also had a sister in Boston who frequently asked Mary to come and stay with her. The nursemaid Biddy continued to live with Mary after Jesse's departure. She had served in the Reno household at Frankford Arsenal and stayed on to help Mary with the baby to be born in February, 1858. Of Biddy, we know only that she was white and apparently came from Philadelphia. Additionally, through Mary's correspondence, we can determine that she and Jesse had numerous friends, including the family physician, Dr. Stone and his wife Margaret. The Stones continued to be good friends and comfort Mary long after Reno's death.

Mary, little Lewis and Biddy all left Frankford Arsenal in mid-July and went to live with her brother William. Mary had hoped that this would be only a temporary arrangement. She hoped to find a rental house of her own, but her house hunting venture apparently did not work out well because, in February, 1858, she was still living at William's home.

Mary was more successful in her efforts to locate a summer resort hotel for herself and her family. In her time, it was customary for affluent Washingtonians to escape the city's steamy summer heat by seeking out cool mountain spas and resorts of one type or another. White Sulphur Springs, then as now, was a favorite of many easterners, and though a number of family and friends were planning to go there in the summer of 1857, Mary desired something less distant and crowded. She settled on Valley View, Virginia, near Warrenton—as she said: "about 4 hours on the cars" [train].

All three, Mary, little Lewis and Biddy, seemed to enjoy the quiet coolness of Valley View. Lewis passed his days "growing fat and playing in the dirt." His mother had to chastise him for leaving the "print of his little teeth in a colored boy's finger." Mary occupied her time by sewing, walking and swinging, while Biddy "caught herself a beau, the only white man on the place."

Marring the idyllic tranquility of Mary's summer retreat was a dream of which she wrote: "I dreamt you were *dead* and woke up in the most intense agony. It was sometime before I could recover from it, and made Biddy get up and light the candle for me. I found myself lying on my back, and remembered besides that I had enjoyed very much some hot flannel cakes for tea - so took care and would not let my fears get the better of me. I hope the next time you visit my dreams it will be in a more agreeable guise. Here I am telling you all my little misadventures, and what are they compared with those you probably meet with daily..."

With the summer over, Mary returned to Washington to anticipate the birth of her baby in February. She regularly attended St. John's Episcopal Church and visited with friends. Also, in response to Reno's request, she made an effort to get his military pay adjusted to that which he was authorized. A brevet officer normally was paid for his regular rank and not his brevet rank. An exception to this rule was made when an officer was serving with a "joint command" made up of more than one department of the service. The Utah expedition qualified Reno to receive captain's pay, and he naturally was desirous of receiving the larger amount. Subsequent correspondence indicated that Mary achieved her mission, and Reno started receiving his increased pay.

The last of Mary's "Utah letters" to which we are privy, was written on March 9, 1858, and deals in large part with the new baby, Alexander. As the proud mother, Mary wrote Jesse that their new son was a good baby, healthy, little trouble, though naturally demanding constant care. She added: "His likeness to yourself is very decided, so of course he must be handsome one of these days, and I only hope he will prove as good as his papa... I discern a likeness to you when smoking your cigar." Pridefully, she went on to say that her brother William laughed at little Alexander's red and ugly face and that she "had to tell him he was better than anything he had produced." At the time of her writing, the baby seemed quite healthy. Unfortunately, Alexander would live only three months and thirteen days.

Mary, herself, seems to sum up the quality of her marriage to Jesse Reno in her first letter to him after he departed for Utah. Poignantly, she wrote: "Last night after you had left us so sadly and I had watched the last glimpse of that carriage which seemed to carry you off so swiftly, I sat a long time thinking—and it was a great comfort to me to reflect that there has never been anything but truth and kindness and love between us —and I offered up a little prayer to God to keep us so always and to make us both to bear our separation cheerfully."

6 — Mount Vernon and Fort Leavenworth

The bittersweet summer of 1859 would bring to Mary Reno the sorrowful loss of her son, Alexander, in May. On the joyful side, however, was the return of her "Darling Jesse" from his unexpectedly long tour of duty in Utah. That assignment ended for Reno on June 25. Also helping to ease her sorrow, would be the relocation to a new and likely exciting area for both Mary and Jesse: he was to be the commander of the arsenal at Mount Vernon, Alabama. Though tensions were growing between the North and the South, there would be a brief time wherein Mary might enjoy her newfound status as the wife of a base commander, living within easy travel to the highly fashionable Mobile, Alabama.

Mount Vernon Arsenal was already well established by the time the Renos moved there, with the original twelve brick buildings having been started in 1830. The entire military reservation encompassed 2,160 acres. The main post of 35 acres was enclosed within a 5,280-foot brick wall which was 16 feet tall and still exists. While the Mount Vernon area is surely verdant, it hardly qualifies as a "mountain", as it rises only 50 feet above the surrounding terrain. Thirty miles north of Mobile and three miles west of the Mobile River, the site of the arsenal does have distinct beauty and, more importantly, was much healthier than the mosquito and fever-ridden surrounding lowlands. For years people down river had sought out Mount Vernon in times of yellow fever epidemics. Of coincidental interest is the fact that a predecessor of Reno was Lieutenant Josiah Gorgas, whose first son was born at the arsenal. That child,

William C. Gorgas, later became surgeon general of the United States, and was renowned, as the conqueror of yellow fever, the very disease so prevalent in the surrounding area.[1] At a later date another notable, though unwilling resident, was Geronimo, along with about 450 of his Apache tribesmen. In the post-Civil War years, the installation continued to grow and eventually became a regimental sized garrison. By 1896 the army had discontinued use of the post and relinquished it to the state of Alabama. Since 1900 it has served as a state mental facility. The commanding officer's house and twelve other original structures are still maintained and utilized.

The commander's residence, just inside the entry gate, was a rather imposing structure. Made of brick and two stories high, it had broad verandas on both levels and numerous windows. Both features provided much desired ventilation in the heat of summer. In the late summer and fall of 1859, the again pregnant Mary, would surely have appreciated the comfort offered by her Mount Vernon house. One would expect that the properly educated Washington, D.C. lady would have been socially acceptable to the local populace and that the mansion-like home of the commander and his wife was the scene of some gracious affairs. With the attendance and assistance of a contract (civilian) physician, Mary gave birth to her son, Conrad, on December 28, 1859. Of the four children she had thus far borne, Conrad would be the first to reach adulthood and live a full life.

Mount Vernon Arsenal was originally established by the federal government to provide ordnance support for the forts and batteries along the Gulf Coast. The first commander had only nine enlisted men in his detachment. These included a carriage maker, armorers, artificers (military mechanics) and laborers. Later his small force was augmented by a blacksmith.[2] In modern military parlance, these men would be considered *support* personnel rather than *combat* troops. A significant function of the men, and particularly the carriages makers, was the constant repair and rebuilding of the wooden gun carriages from the coastal forts. The cannons were unprotected from the weather and were subject to severe deterioration.[3] By Reno's tenure, the arsenal's enlisted detachment had increased to seventeen men. As the needs arose, he likely employed civilian help in addition to the contract physician. Arms were not manufactured at the arsenal but rather, were assembled there from parts brought in from other locations.[4] Although remote and fairly small, Mount Vernon Arsenal maintained a considerable number of small arms and a goodly amount of gunpowder. For the most part, the work would have been routine in nature, and Reno's life would have remained generally blissful on his green hill in Alabama. However, by late 1860 Lincoln had been elected president and South Carolina had seceded from the Union and had seized federal military posts within its territory. The horrors of civil war were but a short time away.

The cry of secession was spreading across the South and Alabamians were near the forefront of the movement. Governor Andrew B. Moore, alerted by the actions of South Carolina and a warning telegram from Georgia's governor, felt compelled to take over Mount Vernon Arsenal and Forts Morgan and Gaines. He justified this action, citing that had he not done so, the United States would have reenforced the military installations. He said this would have left Mobile at the mercy of the ships of war of the United States. He added: "to regain possession of these posts would have cost the State thousands of treasure and the best blood of her sons."[4] That Moore elected to strike Mount Vernon Arsenal during a time of peace with a vastly overwhelming force of four companies of militia might now seem to be a bit of overkill. Reno had only 18 men, most of whom had doubtful combat capabilities.

At dawn on January 4, 1861, and a full week before Alabama seceded from the United States, Moore's four companies of troops scaled the arsenal walls and took complete control of the post. Reno reported to Washington: "I did not make, nor could I have made, any resistance, as they had scaled the walls and taken possession before I knew anything about the movement."[5] Though he had far too few men to even mount guards along the one mile long wall, one might wonder what would have been the result had Reno and his men resisted and been martyrs that morning. Would that have replaced Fort Sumter as the often cited beginning of the coming dreadful conflict? Ten days later while writing to the Alabama House of Representatives, Governor Moore cited his troops for their "galantry" in this action.[6]

In writing to Washington for guidance on January 4, Reno advised that, should he not receive any orders by the 11th, he would discharge any of his men who desired it and leave for the national capital with the remainder.[7] He made no mention of Mary, his children or any other military dependents, so it is not known whether or not they may have gone north earlier. It is doubtful that Reno was given any official forewarning such as modern military forces might receive while in a potentially hostile environment. In present day situations of possible danger, military commanders would be alerted, dependents evacuated and contingency plans put into action. Such preparations at that time would have been virtually impossible, considering the existing insecure chains of command. The future combatants were only beginning to choose up sides, and secret plans would have been entirely subject to compromise. Considering that John B. Floyd, the federal Secretary of War, had strong pro-Southern sentiments and was forced to resign just 7 days earlier,[8] it is readily apparent that, at that time, it would have been difficult to determine who could have been trusted with any Northern plans.

With Mount Vernon Arsenal in Alabama's hands, the federal government lost 22,000 small arms and 150,000 pounds of powder. Brevet Captain Jesse Reno lost his command.

After safely exiting the South, Reno might well have thought he had jumped from the frying pan into the fire on his next assignment. He arrived at Fort Leavenworth, Kansas, to take command of the tenant arsenal there on April 22, 1861. He assumed that function from his prior commander and friend of earlier days at Frankford Arsenal, Major Peter Hagner. Only two days before Reno took over his new command, the ordnance depot at Liberty, Missouri had been seized and looted by a group of armed men.[9] Liberty was just across the river from Leavenworth and the attack on it was

Outer Wall of Mount Vernon Arsenal
Exactly one mile in length and sixteen feet high, this wall was scaled at dawn on January 4, 1861 by four companies of Alabama state troops who captured Jesse Reno, his force of 18 men, and the arsenal. This occurred a week before Alabama seceded from the Union.

Louise McConnell

cause for great alarm to area officials. Reno had arrived at his new post at a time when the situation in neighboring Missouri was extremely volatile. Claiborne Jackson had become governor of that state the previous year and, from the outset, had made it known that his sentiments were with the South. To support his stand, Jackson had raised a militia force named the Minute Men. They were in sore need of arms and Jackson was in the process of planning a takeover of the federal arsenal at St. Louis. However, he was thwarted by the heroic actions of a staunchly pro-Union infantry captain, Nathaniel Lyon.[10] In the meantime, the secessionists attacked the Liberty depot and distributed the arms to "malcontents in the neighborhood."[11]

With such rebellious activities so near by, there was much apprehension in the city of Leavenworth. On April 21, the mayor provided 100 men to augment the military force at the fort that night. Taking over command of the arsenal the next morning, Reno was doubtless no less apprehensive and surely had no wish for a repetition of the Mount Vernon incident. Accordingly, he persuaded the Fort Leavenworth commander, Captain William Steele, to request military assistance from Governor Charles Robinson of Kansas. Robinson provided three companies of 120 militiamen from the town of Leavenworth for the duty. These were known as the Leavenworth Light Infantry, The Union Guards and the Shields Guards. They remained on duty at the fort until relieved eight days later by regular troops brought in to bolster the garrison.[12] Even

House built at Fort Leavenworth under Captain Reno's supervision.

before the incident at Liberty, the federal government had recognized the vulnerability of Fort Leavenworth, and had ordered additional troops there from Forts Kearny, Randall and Ridgely. Colonel Dixon S. Miles of the 2nd Infantry with 165 officers and men from Fort Kearny proceeded to Leavenworth and took command of the main fort on April 30, 1861. With the augmenting force, Fort Leavenworth and its tenant Leavenworth Arsenal would remain securely in the Union camp for the duration of the war. Captain Reno could devote himself to war readiness activities then attendant to all of the arsenals.[13]

Reno inherited an additional duty at the arsenal, when he was ordered to move the "old soldiers burying ground" which had been used since 1827. In order to build a new home for the arsenal commander on the site, the burials were moved to the new National Cemetery. Under his supervision, the home was built on a slight rise at One Scott Street. Overlooking the broad Missouri River, the house was, and still is, an imposing edifice. It is now occupied by a Lieutenant General, commanding the post.

On August 4, 1861, while still at Leavenworth Arsenal, Mary gave birth to the last of the Reno children, Jesse Wilford. This youngest of their children would also live to a full age and eventually achieve fame as an inventor.

With the war obviously well under way by the summer of 1861, Reno appeared to have become somewhat impatient with his rather bland duties at the arsenal and was looking for more active participation in the conflict. His old classmate, Major General George B. McClellan, now headed the Ohio militia and Reno voiced an interest in joining him. On May 9, 1861, McClellan, while requesting other support from General-in-Chief Winfield Scott, then commanding the Union army, asked that Captain Reno be assigned to him as his ordnance officer.[14] Nothing came of this request however, because shortly thereafter McClellan continued his meteoric rise and moved east to bigger assignments. Whether or not this was fortuitous for Reno can only be speculated.

Reno's wait for more exciting duty, however, was not to be long. In the fall of 1861, Brigadier General Ambrose E. Burnside was recruiting troops and selecting officers for his expedition to North Carolina. For his primary assistants, Burnside chose three of his close friends of academy days: John G. Foster, John Parke and Jesse L. Reno. Burnside had all three men promoted to the rank of brigadier general of volunteers. Each would later fully justify his faith in their abilities. Once again, Reno was off to war.

7— WITH BURNSIDE IN NORTH CAROLINA

Command of the Union army was bestowed on Major General George B. McClellan in 1861. While he often had obvious shortcomings as a battlefield leader, he was highly intelligent and was an excellent planner and organizer. He had the ability to draw around him men of great potential as leaders.

In their continuing efforts to effect a blockade of Confederate ports on the Atlantic, Federal military leaders decided to mount a major amphibious attack against Roanoke Island and other nearby targets. In addition to supporting the North's blockade of the coast, the Roanoke attack offered other sound reasons for the action. McClellan was planning an inland campaign against Richmond and he calculated that the coastal action would draw some of the southern troops away from him. Further, the taking of key sites in the coastal area would help interdict some Confederate supply lines and he hoped, weaken Virginia to the point of submission. McClellan also felt that should he be successful in taking Richmond, the Union force on the coast could move inland and join him. Another reason for the planned Roanoke campaign was the belief by some in Washington that loyalist sentiment was strong in North Carolina and a successful occupation of the coast might change that state's allegiance.

Accordingly, in September of 1861, McClellan directed his friend, Brigadier General Ambrose Burnside, to recruit 15,000 men, to be known as the Coastal Division, and to assemble and train them at Annapolis, Maryland. Burnside, like McClellan, looked to his close friends for support and selected John G. Foster, John G. Parke and Jesse L. Reno to be his three brigade commanders. Each was promoted to brigadier general of volunteers. In Jesse Reno's case, he would never hold the ranks of major, lieutenant colonel or colonel. Though quantum jumps in officer rank in the present time might seem unique, such promotions then were a normal procedure. The Union desperately needed senior officers as leaders and almost the only men with the necessary qualifications were military academy graduates. Thus, it was not uncommon for lieutenants and captains to become colonels or generals overnight. Often friendship played a big part in their rapid elevation and top leaders chose men they knew and trusted to serve under them. It is not surprising, therefore, that McClellan, Burnside, Reno, Foster and Parke, all with overlapping cadet years and knowing each other well, would be drawn together.

Almost immediately after promotion to general, Reno took advantage of his new rank and sent for his younger brother Frank to serve as his aide-de-camp. Benjamin Franklin Reno, usually known as "BF" or "Frank", was seven years younger than Jesse and was living in Marengo, Iowa, at the outbreak of the Civil War. Though he was in his early thirties, Frank did not marry until the close of the war. While still in Iowa, he had organized Company H of the 2nd Iowa Cavalry, made up of men from Johnson and Iowa Counties. Originally, Frank was appointed a second lieutenant, but before joining Reno in Maryland, he had been promoted to first lieutenant. Frank served faithfully as his brother's aide until the latter's death.[1]

Newly promoted Brigadier General Reno left his assignment at Leavenworth Arsenal on December 9 and reported to headquarters in Washington, D.C. ten days later. He was immediately instructed to report to the Coastal Division at Annapolis. He complied with the order on the following day, December 20.[2] Available information does not indicate whether Mary Reno and their three boys accompanied Jesse to Washington, but it is reasonable to assume she did so, since that city had been her family's home. It is also comforting to think that Reno may have been able to spend his last Christmas with his family.

Taking command of his 2nd Brigade at the camp outside Annapolis, Reno found he would be leading five northeastern volunteer infantry regiments: the 21st Massachusetts, 51st New York, 51st Pennsylvania, 9th New Jersey and 6th New Hampshire. With only a few weeks to train the new recruits, most of the time was necessarily spent on the rudiments of soldiering, omitting desirable training for amphibious landing.[3] Considering the size of Burnside's Division and the overall scope of the operation that would require a

Benjamin Franklin Reno
1830–1908
Younger brother and aide-de-camp of General Jesse Reno. He was generally called "BF" or "Frank".

Mary Jane Powell, B. F. Reno's granddaughter

tremendous fleet of transports and protective vessels, the organizational phase proceeded well under the time constraints.

By early January, 1862, the Burnside expedition was ready to be on its way. Likely, few major Civil War operations were as well-kept secrets as the planned attack along the North Carolina coast. The obviously large-scale operation under way at Annapolis, as well as the massive armada gathered there, had Washington and other areas buzzing. There could be no doubt that the South, as well, was deeply concerned about what was in the wind.

Newspapers were clamoring to find out where the big attack would come, but for a time well after the ships had embarked, there were perhaps no more than six persons in the entire country who knew the actual destination of the expedition. Reno was one of them.[4] President Lincoln was later attributed with relating a story of the pressures exerted to ascertain the mission of the Burnside expedition. A prominent senator called on the president and virtually demanded that he be advised of the details of the expedition. After resisting his entrearies for a while, Lincoln finally said: "Now I will tell you in great confidence where they are going, if you will promise not to speak of it to any one." "You may rely upon my discretion," responded the statesman, in his most impressive tones.

"Well now, my friend," said Lincoln, "the expedition is going to sea." The senator took his hat and left in speechless rage.[5]

On the order of General Burnside, troops started loading on the ships on January 5, with the last unit, the 6th New Hampshire, boarding on the morning of January 8. On the morning of the next day, all set sail with orders to rendezvous at Fort Monroe, Virginia. A member of the 25th Massachusetts described the departure in an article for the *National Tribune*, a military newspaper:

"On the morning of January 9, 1862, at 8 a.m., the expedition comprising 117 vessels, moved out of the harbor of Annapolis. It was grandest sight ever seen before upon this side of the Atlantic."

The steamer *New Brunswick*, having on board the 10th Connecticut, led the way, followed in two lines by the remainder of the fleet. From all the vessels and steamers the most enthusiastic cheers were heard, mingled with the music of a dozen or more regimental bands. It was a beautiful morning as the fleet sailed so grandly into the waters of the Chesapeake. The long-talked-of expedition was moving, the last letter had been mailed for home, and into thousands of dwellings dotting the country would soon go the messengers of affection, bearing the last farewell of many a brave soldier moving upon his last expedition upon earth. As the news of the movement of the fleet sped swiftly over the land, there were thousands of throbbing hearts and many a silent prayer went up from the homes of soldiers for the safety and success of the expedition.

Its destination was unknown even to the officers of the fleet, and the grand question discussed on the transports was: Where are we going, where shall we land and where strike the blow. The sailing masters had only one direction—"Follow the leading vessel," and the master of the leading vessel moved under sealed orders. The Confederates showed the same ignorance concerning the place of destination. Magruder was in a frenzy at Yorktown; Beauregard was awaiting it at New Orleans, and at Norfolk the excitement of expectation was unrelieved by a single item of information."[6]

The brief journey from Annapolis to the rendezvous point at Fort Monroe at Hampton Roads, Virginia, was unencumbered by weather, and the formidable force was able to assemble and take on fuel and supplies without great problems. The fleet, under the overall direction of Flag Officer Louis Goldsborough was, indeed, an imposing array of vessels. They included 20 light-draught ships with over 50 guns on board; 7 gunboats; and nearly 40 transports, each capable of carrying 400–500 men. Additionally, there were 50 smaller boats to carry supplies and rations for sixty days.[7]

At 9:30 on the night of January 11, the expeditionary force left Hampton Roads. General Reno travelled on the *Northerner* with the 21st Massachusetts. Sealed envelopes with secret orders were opened and the ships' commanders learned that they were to continue south along the coast, progressing past Nag's Head and Cape Hatteras and ultimately, on to Hatteras Inlet. The good weather that had thus far benevolently abetted the Burnside expedition came to an end; on January 13, while off Hatteras, a regular Atlantic gale came up. Though most of the ships had arrived in the area, the violence of the storm precluded any movement beyond their anchored position at the mouth of the inlet. For the better part of two days, both men and ships suffered the battering of the gale. Two or three ships were driven on to sand bars or ashore and destroyed along with their cargo. But overall, the results of the storm were far less than catastrophic. Another storm hit the area between January 22 and 24, and this also delayed the expedition's entrance into the inland approaches to their real goal, Roanoke Island.

Coping with the foul weather was not the only problem posed by nature at this point of the endeavor. Unsealed orders revealed that the armada was to go through the Hatteras Inlet but, unfortunately, many of the vessels drew more than the seven and a half feet of water available there. Thus, the laborious task of shifting men and supplies from ship to ship, in order to float the vessels over the shallow inlet caused a significant delay and provided a warning to the Confederate defenders in the area. Some of the larger ships were unable to make the passage and were sent back to Annapolis. For lack of sufficient transports, three regiments were offloaded at Hatteras and lost to the coming campaign. The 6th New Hampshire, assigned to Reno, was one of those units left behind. General Parke's greatly diminished 3rd Brigade was, however, augmented by the 9th New York (Hawkins' Zouaves) of the Hatteras garrison.[8] This regiment would later, while temporarily under his command, cause major problems for Reno.

Finally overcoming the forces of nature, the ships weighed anchor at 9:00 on the morning of February 7. The area was clear of fog and Burnside had given the order to progress to Roanoke Island. The waterway was defended by seven small Confederate gunboats but these were quickly forced into retreat by Goldsborough's overwhelming armada. Other than some ineffective cannonading from defending artillery on the island, Burnside's troops met with little opposition to their landing.

The Confederate forces in the area were under the command of the former governor of Virginia, Brigadier General Henry A. Wise, but he was ill at the time at Nag's Head and was unable to participate in the island's defense. In his place, Colonel H. M. Shaw of the 8th North Carolina would attempt to cope with the attackers. Unfortunately for Shaw, he was vastly outnumbered and was unable to slow the inevitable conquest of Roanoke Island. Squabbling between the central government at Richmond and South Carolina's governor Henry T. Clark over the issue of who should provide additional forces for the area, had left Roanoke Island with only token military defenses. When it became apparent to Confederate leaders that the island was Burnside's target, there were barely 1,600 southern troops stationed there. Early on the morning of February 7, these were augmented by ten regiments of the Wise Legion, but Colonel Shaw's force never numbered more than 2,500 defenders. Despite their valiant efforts, they were no match for the more than 12,000 Union men Burnside put on the island, nor were they able to bear the pounding they received from Goldsborough's shipboard cannons.[9]

After assessing the terrain and defenses, Burnside elected to make the landing at Ashley's Harbor, about halfway up the western shore of Roanoke Island. Starting about three in the afternoon of February 7, his troops began to wade ashore through waist-deep water and mud for a quarter of a mile. This was necessary because the shallowness of the water prohibited the small boats from landing. A heavy rainstorm added to the discomfort on the extremely cold night.[10] Sleep was difficult for the miserably wet and chilled Northerners, but for most, this was their first military venture and

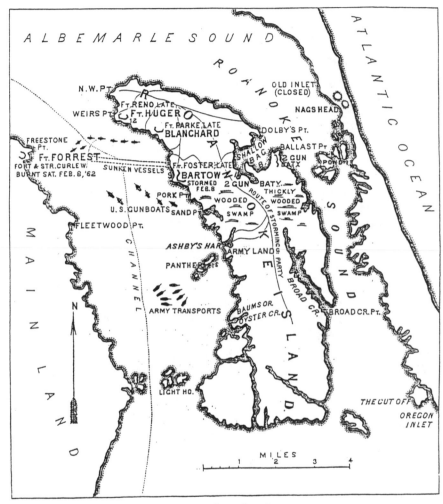

Roanoke Island

they bore up well to their task. By 7:00 the following morning Burnside had established his line of battle. It consisted of three columns which were to proceed north through the center of the island. General Foster's brigade led in the middle, with Reno's four regiments on the left and Parke's on the right. The only route available to the north was a quagmire of a road running generally near the center of the island. On either side were heavily timbered swamps. About a mile and a half north from the Union landing point, the Confederates had thrown a defensive line across much of the island and at right angles to the road. Bolstering the center of their line, the southerners had an earthwork mounting three guns. This defensive line proved to be the site of the primary battlefield for Roanoke Island.

Foster, leading the attack in the center, was soon halted by withering fire from the Southerners crouched behind their lines; to proceed further along the narrow corridor in a frontal attack appeared suicidal. Meanwhile, Reno and his 2nd Brigade had caught up with Foster's stalled troops. Looking over the situation, Reno suggested to Foster that the 2nd Brigade might be able to move through the supposedly impenetrable swamp on the left and surprise the enemy on his right flank. Foster, the senior of the two, approved the plan and Reno moved out at the head of his leading regiment, the 21st Massachusetts. The swamp was indeed thick and muddy and Reno's efforts would require nearly two hours, but in the end, his troops came storming toward the much surprised right end of the Confederate line.

At this point, Reno is reported to have turned to Lieutenant Colonel Alberto Maggi, commander of the 21st Massachusetts, and asked "Colonel Maggi, can you take that battery?" "We can, General," was Maggi's reply. Reno gave him the word to go ahead.[11] Thus the men of the 21st were first on the three-gun parapet, capturing the enemy's colors and hoisting their own regimental flag. Moments later, the 51st Pennsylvania was beside them, running up the national flag.

Taking advantage of Reno's shock to the Confederate right, Foster had been able to launch a coordinated frontal attack, with the 9th New York Zouaves in the lead. The Confederate defenders were put to flight. Except for mop-up operations, the battle for Roanoke Island was over. The flamboyant Colonel Rush Hawkins took credit for his 9th New York being the first to enter and take the parapet, and relegated the actions of Reno's men to a mere supporting function.[12] This may well have been the source of a Hawkins-Reno rhubarb that flourished later in the campaign. With the loss of their primary line of defense, the southerners retreated pell-mell back to their cantonment areas on the north end of the island, there hoping to be evacuated by their ships. Reno's 2nd Brigade led the chase, soon to be followed by Foster's brigade. The beleaguered Confederates soon learned that no ships were available to come to their rescue, and it was apparent that surrender was the only reasonable alternative. Reno accepted the surrender of Colonel J. K. Jordan and his 31st North Carolina Regiment, numbering about 500 officers and men.

Under a flag of truce, General Foster accepted the unconditional surrender of the remaining Confederates on the island.[13] In addition to 2,500 captured prisoners, the southern force lost 24 killed and 68 wounded. Among those killed was General Wise's son, Captain O. Jennings Wise. The Union victory also yielded five forts with 32 guns, winter quarters for 4,000 troops, hospital buildings and a stand of 3,000 small arms.[14] Union losses were 41 killed and 227 wounded. Reno reported his loss at 15 dead and 79 wounded. His dead, along with the other Union men killed on the island, were buried in a small fenced plot with solemn services conducted by Chaplain Horace James with appropriate music furnished by Gilmore's band of the 24th Massachusetts.

For the still living, the evening after the battle was one of camaraderie. Confederate prisoners were fed their evening meal first. Later, men in both blue and grey sat smoking their pipes around the campfires, discussing the events of the day and speculating as to what the future might bring. A Southern officer, nineteen year-old Lieutenant Colonel Burgwyn had lost his diary on the battlefield that day. He would later escape by boat. He too would meet his fate on a Maryland promotory called South Mountain in the coming September.[15]

In his after action report to General Burnside, Reno characteristically gave great credit for the success to his subordinates, especially his regimental commanders. In passing out laurels, he did not overlook his aides including brother Frank.[16] Jesse Reno also received his share of glory in a communication from Burnside:

The general commanding congratulates his troops on their brilliant and successful occupation of Roanoke Island. The courage and steadiness they have shown under fire is what he expected of them, and he accepts it as a token of future victory.

Each regiment on the island will inscribe its banner "Roanoke Island, February 8, 1862." The highest praise is due Brigadier-Generals Foster, Reno, and Parke, who so bravely and energetically carried out the movement that has resulted in the complete success of the Union arms.[17]

With his first objective achieved, Burnside could make plans for moving on to his second target, North Carolina's major port, the town of New Bern on the Atlantic and North Carolina Railroad. Since Roanoke Island was now in Union hands, there was no great urgency for speedy action. The Coastal Division could rather leisurely occupy the abandoned barracks of the departed rebels and refortify the island. This process took Burnside's ground troops a little over a month to accomplish. In the meantime, his naval arm cleared Albemarle Sound and adjoining waterways of all Confederate seagoing resistance. The so-called rebel "mosquito fleet" of seven gunboats was soon rendered ineffective and the Union armada had free rein to assault shore targets.

On February 12, leaving Colonel Hawkins behind to command Roanoke Island with his 9th New York and three other regiments, Burnside set sail for New Bern on the Neuse River. Reno and part of his command were aboard the side-wheeler transport *Patuxent*.[18] Anchoring eighteen miles south of New Bern that evening, the federal troops waited until the following morning to go ashore. On the 13th, the Yankees trudged north through rain and mud, unencumbered by any significant enemy harassment. In many respects, the coming scene would be a replay of the Roanoke Island assault.

The Confederate defenders of New Bern, under the command of Brigadier General Lawrence O. Branch, elected to establish their main battle line in a generally east-west direction about five miles below the town. The mile-long works, known as the Fort Thompson line, was anchored at the east end on the Neuse River bank with a battery of thirteen guns, and on the opposite side by a line of redoubts. Branch's line of works were defended by eight regiments of infantry, five hundred cavalrymen, and three batteries of artillery, each with six guns.[19]

As in the action at Roanoke Island, Jesse Reno's brigade was on the Union left as it marched north to confront the defenders. This time, however, his men had better terrain to traverse. Instead of having to move through woods as did other brigades, Reno's men followed the railroad bed of the Atlantic and North Georgia. Again with the 21st Massachusetts Regiment in the lead, Reno's 2nd Brigade would be the first to make contact with the enemy line. Foster's brigade was moving up on the center and right and Parke's brigade was held in reserve in the center. Marching to within less than a mile of the enemy breastwork, and hindered by rain, Burnside's troops called a halt and attempted to rest during the night of the February 13. At the next dawn, with morning fog blanketing the area, the Union attackers were on the move. The first engagement took place about 8:00 a.m. Although outnumbered by a ratio of nearly 3 to 1, the Confederates, behind the relative safety of breastworks, could render severe damage to the Union forces. At about 9:00 in the morning, Reno ordered a charge by the 21st Massachusetts at his end of the line. He personally accompanied the 21st as it went over the enemy breastworks. Later he faced a countercharge by two Rebel regiments and was driven back.[20] Vicious fighting continued all along the line for nearly three more hours.

Finally, with overwhelming and combined efforts of the three Union brigades, the Confederate line broke and fell back. Closely pursued by the Federal troops, Branch's North Carolinians fled through New Bern and over the Trent River, burning the bridges behind them. For the most part, they utilized trains to retreat inland toward Goldsboro. Their loss of equipment and supplies was significant. Besides the port city, they gave up 64 guns, two steamboats, a number of sailing vessels, a large quantity of ammunition and considerable amounts of other quartermaster stores. Although most of the Confederates were able to escape, more than two hundred were taken prisoner. The Union loss was placed at 91 killed and 466 wounded.[21] Burnside could once again put a check mark beside an objective of his campaign.

A few days after his success at New Bern, Burnside started action against his third objective, Beaufort Harbor and its protective Fort Macon. He dispatched General Parke and his 3rd Brigade south to lay siege to the fort. This would further tighten his hold on the North Carolina coast and provide an additional port area for receiving supplies from the north. While Parke went off to ultimately capture Fort Macon, Reno's and Foster's brigades were busy building trenches around New Bern and otherwise reenforcing the area. Fort Totten was also built, in an effort to make the captured area as impregnable as possible.

Although Burnside probably wanted to make other major thrusts inland and to the south, he lacked sufficient troops to risk such an endeavor. He did, however, order one further brief expedition. His naval chief, Commodore Rowan, feared that the Confederates might send ironclad vessels against his wooden fleet by way of a canal from Norfolk. To support Rowan, Burnside drew up orders for his ground-based troops to attack the enemy and destroy the locks on the Dismal Swamp Canal. These were located at South Mills, considerably north on the Pasquotank River.[22] Realizing that such a thrust in the direction of Norfolk would likely draw major enemy reenforcements, Burnside planned a quick strike on the target, with his troops to return to their transporting ships soon after the foray. Reno was ordered to lead the expedition.

As directed by Burnside, Reno's raiding party was made up of five regiments, totaling somewhat over 3,000 men. He took his own 21st Massachusetts and 51st Pennsylvania from New Bern, then picked up Colonel Hawkins and his three regiments at Roanoke Island. In later years, Hawkins took credit for initiating the mission and for its limited success. He exposed his vanity by stating his surprise that Reno was put in command. Likely, Hawkins was expecting to have that honor and was miffed at being passed over.[23] It can only be speculated that this slight to his personal ambitions may have influenced Hawkins to take rash and costly actions that brought only partial success to the assigned mission.

On the night of April 18, Reno's raiding force was conveyed up Albemarle Sound and the Pasquotank River to a point about three miles below Elizabeth City. They disembarked at the small community of Chantilly. Coincidentally, some four and a half months later Reno would fight another battle at another tiny community in Virginia with the uncommon name of Chantilly. The first troops, including Reno with Hawkins' three regiments, the 9th and 89th New York and the 6th New Hampshire, arrived at the Chantilly landing about midnight. The remaining two regiments from Massachusetts and Pennsylvania were delayed because their transport vessels were grounded at the mouth of the river and did not reach the planned anchorage until 7:00 the next morning. By 3 a.m. all of Hawkins' men were ashore. Not wishing to entirely lose the element of surprise and allow the enemy ample time for defensive preparation, Reno directed Hawkins to move his troops by the quickest route to South Mills and there secure the locks until Reno could bring up the remaining two regiments.

Although Hawkins had been ordered by Reno to proceed directly to a bridge near South Mills, Hawkins allowed himself to be duped by a local guide.[24] Rather than taking the well-known and direct route to South Mills, he followed the misdirection of the local man and marched his troops on a circuitous route a full ten miles out of the way. Not only did Hawkins' blunder delay the strike by about four hours and lose the advantage of surprise, it also fatigued his men.[25] Finally, some twelve miles north of their debarkation point, at about 11:00 in the morning, Hawkins was able to join Reno and the other two regiments. By this time, the 3rd Georgia Regiment, under the command of Colonel Ambrose Wright, was able to establish a strong defensive line about one and a half miles below South Mills. Although Wright had only 400 men to face Reno's 3,000, he was able to select an advantageous position for his troops at the wooded north end of a large clearing. He also had a cavalry company for reconnaissance and four cannons to counter Reno's four guns. With this force, Colonel Wright and his Georgians would be able to make a strong stand.

Reno, observing that a frontal attack through the open clearing would be unnecessarily costly to the lives of his men, ordered the 21st Massachusetts and the 51st Pennsylvania to veer to the right into the pine woods and approach the Confederates' left flank. Likewise, he directed the 6th New Hampshire to conduct a similar move by going to the left through the woods. Hawkins, with the 9th and 89th New York Regiments, had halted at the rear. Reno found Hawkins and ordered him to follow the first two regiments to the right, through the woods, and help attack the enemy's left flank.

Hawkins failed to follow this order, later claiming that the woods were swampy and impenetrable; this despite the fact that the 21st Massachusetts and 51st Pennsylvania had already traversed the area with no great difficulty.[26]

Subsequent fighting was furious and several Union attacks were repulsed by the meager Confederate force. Once again, not following Reno's orders, the flamboyant Hawkins was duped when he mistook a lull in their firing to be a weakness in the center of the rebel line. On his own volition, he ordered his 9th New York Zouaves to make a fixed bayonet charge across the open clearing against the Confederate center. This rash action was repulsed with disastrous results and Hawkins' survivors fled into the woods. His ill-conceived act cost Hawkins 75 of his men and a wound in his arm.

Finally, the overwhelming strength of the other three regiments following Reno's orders to flank the enemy, coupled with the Georgians running low on ammunition, enabled the Union men to turn the rebel flanks and force their retreat. No pursuit was attempted since the Union soldiers, especially Hawkins' men, were near total exhaustion. Ammunition was now also running low for the Northerners and Reno correctly anticipated that strong Confederate reenforcements would be dispatched from Norfolk. Additionally, Reno was under orders to make only a brief foray against South Mills and quickly return to his transports. Therefore, Reno rested his troops, returned to the transport ships, and sailed back to Roanoke Island. Fortunately, the targeted but undestroyed canal locks would pose no future problem for the North, for the canal was never used to convey any attacking Confederate armored vessels.

Hawkins' disobedience of orders and the resultant qualified success of the mission would lead to a rash of reports from both him and Reno, and a wide disparity between their respective accounts of what really happened. Hawkins, contrary to military regulation, bypassed Reno and made his after-action report directly to Burnside. As he did after Roanoke Island, he took credit for routing the Confederates when, in fact, it was his faulty directions that led to the limited success. Other than the 6th New Hampshire, which was, in reality, operating under Reno's direction, Hawkins failed to mention or give any credit to the real victors of the conflict. Though not actually stated, he clearly implied that it was Reno's fault for not continuing on and destroying the locks.[27]

Reno was not reluctant to show anger and disdain in the face of what he considered military ignorance or vainglorious actions and, in this case, sent Burnside three scathing reports countering Colonel Hawkins' exaggerated and biased accounts. Additionally, Reno virtually demanded that General Burnside issue an order setting the record straight and exonerating him. Burnside complied by issuing General Orders No. 30 on April 26.[28] He further supported Reno when he submitted his report to Secretary of War Edwin Stanton on April 29.[29]

Reno, as with a number of the skilled regular officers of the Civil War, on occasion had difficulty accepting the self-seeking and flamboyant actions of some of the politically appointed state volunteer officers. In this regard, he was, like many of the more successful leaders, considered a stern taskmaster. A very few latter-day writers have implied that Reno was unfeeling and perhaps a bit of a martinet. More correctly, one outstanding modern historian has described Reno as "a determined no-nonsense regular".[30] Surely, when it came to the gory business of fighting wars Reno had a low level of tolerance for life-costing ignorance or personal aggrandizement among his subordinates. Yet, with rare exceptions, the unit histories of most of the regiments which fought under Reno later reflected sincere respect for his leadership and a deep admiration for his talents. Hawkins' opportunistic ways were of course a thorn in Reno's side. In his two years of Civil War service, Hawkins seemed to have had trouble taking orders and otherwise getting along with other superiors. Prior to the Burnside expedition, he had been relieved of command of Hatteras Inlet for minor setbacks there, and was under threat of arrest by the new commander. Later, while leading a brigade at Fredericksburg, his reckless and disastrous assaults caused him to get into new trouble with Burnside.[31]

On July 3, 1862, Burnside's venture into North Carolina ended. He, with part of General Parke's brigade and Reno's command, moved north to Fort Monroe and thence to new exploits in Virginia.

8— WITH POPE IN VIRGINIA

It was Reno's misfortune that his entire Civil War service occurred during a time when Lincoln was unsuccessfully groping to find a truly effective leader for the Union army in the East. In the summer of 1862, Reno participated in his only major Civil War battle, Bull Run. That Reno would acquit himself most admirably in that battle could not alter the fact that he would be forced to share the humiliating defeat caused by the incompetence of one leading Northern general, John Pope, and the delaying of another, George McClellan.

As indicated in the previous chapter, the Burnside expedition to North Carolina could be considered overall a success. McClellan's peninsular campaign, however, could not lay claim to such an achievement. McClellan, because of his delay and failure to take action when he had the advantage, was defeated in the Seven Days Battle, failed in his goal to take Richmond and fell back to Harrisons Landing to lick his wounds and rest.

In Washington, D.C., patience had worn thin with "Little Mac" and Lincoln sought to replace him. Major General John Pope was brought east from Missouri, where he had achieved moderate success, to head a new command to be eventually known as the Army of Virginia. This newly designated force was initially made by consolidating several independent commands in or near Washington. Since there were now two Union armies on the East coast, one commanded by Pope and the other by McClellan, the question of overall control had to be resolved. Lincoln brought the bookish and overcautious Major General Henry W. Halleck from the western area to the capital to be general-in-chief. Halleck's talents proved to be more effective as a staff or "desk officer" than as a field commander, but his appointment gave Lincoln a more or less graceful means of diluting McClellan's power. Further downgrading of McClellan was achieved by siphoning off some of his troops and adding them to Pope's army. Reno and his expanded command were part of that augmentation.

McClellan's unsuccessful move on Richmond not only caused displeasure in Washington but also necessitated the drawing up of new battle plans, both for the defense of the capital and offensive action against Richmond. Pope's new Army of Virginia made several minor thrusts southward in Virginia, taking the community of Culpeper Court House in mid-July, but with few other successes. In late July, Halleck arrived in Washington to assume his new post as general-in-chief and soon realized the need to extricate McClellan from the Peninsula and bring his forces up in close support of Pope's troops in northern Virginia. Halleck's initial plan of action called for Pope to make feigning thrusts southward from Culpeper toward and possibly across the Rapidan River, as though to move on Richmond. This, he felt, would relieve some of the Confederate pressure on the Union forces on the Peninsula and allow McClellan to expeditiously withdraw north and link up with Pope. There, with the resultant overwhelming strength, Halleck could realistically hope for a successful drive on Richmond.[1] To his misfortune, and the North's, neither friend nor foe cooperated with his plans.

McClellan, for his part, was far from "expeditious" in his withdrawal. This ultimately denied the Union its potentially dominant strength at the coming Second Battle of Bull Run.[2] General Robert E. Lee also was not of a mind to provide any support to Halleck's plans. Lee quickly observed the threat posed by the Union if Pope and McClellan's armies were to be allowed to join forces. Further, Lee correctly ascertained that McClellan was reluctant to move and was no longer a real threat on the Peninsula. Seeing a possibility of destroying each of the two Union armies if he could hit them before they could unite, Lee dispatched Major General Jackson north to confront Pope's army.[3] The ensuing battle at Cedar Mountain, on August 9, saw Jackson's forces halting the Union thrusts to the south and driving Pope back to the northern side of the Rappahannock River. Meanwhile, Lee left only a token force on the Peninsula to face McClellan and moved most of the remainder of his army, under Major General James Longstreet, north to support Jackson on August 13. With the reconstituting of his army, Lee had a force superior to Pope's Army of Virginia and with this, Lee hoped for a

58

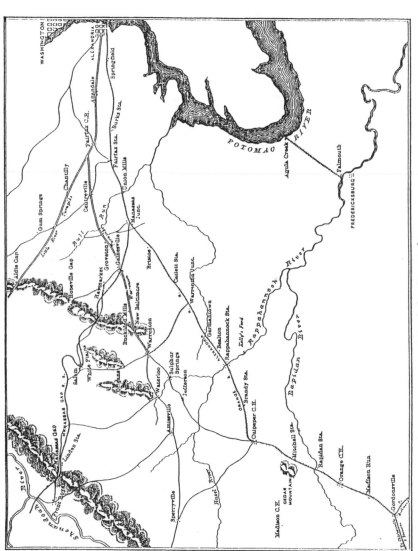

Virginia Campaign

The Army Under Pope (1881)

quick and decisive victory over Pope at the Rappahannock.[4] It was into this melee that Jesse Reno was ordered.

Coming north from successes in North Carolina, Burnside's IX Corps disembarked at Aquia Creek, north of Fredericksburg, Virginia, then moved south to Falmouth. Burnside stayed in that area but dispatched, on August 12, Reno's and Stevens' divisions north to join with Pope.[5] Reno, promoted to major general on July 12, was put in command of both of these two IX Corps divisions, a force totalling about 8,000 men. Two days later, on August 14, Reno arrived at the base of the Blue Ridge Mountains to become a part of Pope's army. Lee had hoped, as already mentioned, to quickly defeat Pope along the Rappahannock and had made plans to launch a surprise attack on the Union forces on August 18. For one of the few times in his Eastern campaign, General Pope received and correctly interpreted intelligence information which would allow him to take evasive action and foil Lee's planned attack.[6] Subsequently, the river became swollen with rains and this further hindered Lee's ability to get at Pope's forces. To overcome what might be an extended stalemate, with each of the combatants holding to their respective sides of the river, Lee developed an alternate plan which sent Jackson and his men north around the Union right flank to come in on their rear.[7] This action, as Lee correctly surmised, drew the Federals away from their secure position along the Rappahannock.

The often cited "brother-against-brother", "friend-against-friend" aspect of the Civil War was brought out most vividly and ironically with the fact that Reno's forces would, in the brief span of only two weeks, be pitted directly against the troops of Stonewall Jackson on three different occasions. First, Reno was ordered to chase Jackson through northern Virginia on a hare-and-hound operation; secondly, he would be directly opposed to Jackson at the Second Battle of Bull Run; and finally, they would confront each other at the Battle of Chantilly. That these two men, both originally from West Virginia, classmates at West Point and, moreover, once good friends, should be thrown at each other so often in such a short period of time seems especially poignant. When considering that more than sixty generals, North and South, were engaged in the Second Battle of Bull Run, the coincidence of Jesse Reno and Tom Jackson being positioned directly against each other stretches the imagination.

Lee's plan to send Jackson north on a flanking movement around the Union army was not without risk. Any time when an army commander divides his force there is an inherent danger that he could be attacked while in a diminished status. This, however, was not the only time that General Lee divided his army and placed his trust in the brilliant tactician Jackson. Lee calculated that General Pope would take the bait and chase after Jackson, thus dividing the Union army. Lee also envisaged getting behind Pope's troops and cutting off his main supply line at Manasass Junction. Pope did, in fact, take the bait, thinking he saw a chance to annihilate Jackson. Even to the evening of the last day of the Second Battle of Bull Run some four days later, Pope appeared to hold to a fixation that he was on the brink of trapping and destroying the elusive Stonewall Jackson. The subsequent reality would be that the roles of hare and hound were reversed and Pope turned out to be the trapped rabbit.

Reno's was one of three commands dispatched by Pope to pursue Jackson. While Jesse Reno would later have better success against his old chum, Tom Jackson, on this occasion he was totally stymied. Jackson was not to be found and stopped until he, himself, was ready to stop at the old Bull Run battlefield. There he dug in and became the bait for Lee's plan to entrap Pope and the Federal forces.[8]

Jackson's planning for the mission was well conceived and his actions were more than a challenge for Pope. Before starting, Jackson stripped his troops of all but the most necessary equipment and supplies. His soldiers travelled light and carried a three-day supply of cooked rations. Perhaps contributing as much to his success of this lightened and highly mobile force, was his thorough concern for secrecy. Only one man, and that man was Jackson himself, knew the destination of his troops. He did not confide this information even to his three division commanders; determined that no error or lost orders would divulge his intentions. As his officers reached each destination en route, they were given new instructions for the next leg of their march.[9]

Pope was totally confounded by Jackson's wily ways and directed Reno's movements ineffectively. This caused unnecessary fatigue for his troops.[10] Whether Reno would have been more successful in catching Jackson, if left to his own judgement in moving his troops, can only be speculated. In any case, Stonewall Jackson carried out his mission with complete success. Under the cover of secrecy, he marched his three divisions 62 miles in forty-eight hours. At that point, he raided the Union supply base at Manassas Junction, effectively cutting off Pope's lines of supply as well as communications.[11] By the time Pope found out what had happened and directed troops to Manassas, Jackson's men had glutted themselves on a wide variety of delicacies, decimated the remaining food and ordnance, and moved on. His destination, as already mentioned, was on the western edge of the Bull Run battlefield. With his line of battle oriented generally north and south, he dug in and waited.

Reno's force moved into a position opposite and to the east of Jackson. These positions set the scene for the Second Battle of Bull Run.

The Second Bull Run battle took place on August 29 and 30, 1862. There was preliminary fighting near Gainesville and Groveton before the main action, and subsequent fighting at Chantilly; all of which could be considered a part of the overall battle. Pope, by August 28, had brought up the bulk of his army and had them arrayed before Jackson's numerically inferior Confederates. Pope's movements were not without confusion and suffering, for Jackson's earlier raid on Manassas Junction was taking its toll on both Union men and animals for lack of supplies. Pope's intelligence information also suffered from the communication interdiction achieved by Jackson. Despite his hardships, however, Pope had illusions that he could attack and destroy Jackson. The battle began in earnest around noon on August 29 with Reno's portion of the IX Corps at the heart of the struggle. His force, other than four regiments held in reserve, was fighting the center of Jackson's line. As the day wore on, Reno's men, along with those of Major General Philip Kearney, were meeting with a fair amount of success in pushing back Jackson's Confederates. Had Pope's strategy of bringing other units against Jackson's right flank or southern end succeeded during the afternoon, Jackson might well have been crushed. Unfortunately, Pope's flanking movement was not carried out. Major General Fitz-John Porter was later blamed for not attacking Jackson's right flank and was later court-martialed for what Pope considered insubordination. Twenty-three years later Porter was exonerated. However, for the time, the chance for defeating Jackson was lost.

At 5:30 in the evening, a disgruntled Pope ordered Reno, Kearney and others to make a frontal attack on Jackson. The ensuing fighting by both sides was desperate and gallant, and could be considered a tribute to the leadership of both Reno and Jackson. At sunset, Jesse Reno had prevailed, held his position and driven Jackson's men back into the woods on the western side of the original battlefield. The Confederate dead and wounded were left behind. As darkness fell, the first day of the battle could be judged a victory for the Federal forces.[12] Pope likely closed out the day with thoughts that he had Jackson trapped and ready for the kill. Whether these thoughts blinded him and impaired his judgement the following day has been debated by Civil War scholars ever since.

During the night of August 29–30, Lee brought up the remainder of his troops and by noon on August 30, his forces outnumbered Pope's. The Union army made a determined stand until Lee threw the other half of his army, under Major General James Longstreet, into the fray. Longstreet attacked from the south, hit-ting Pope directly on his left flank, while Jackson kept up the frontal attack. Longstreet also was supported by a large artillery component. The murderous enfilading bombardment it launched, coupled with the ground attack from two directions, proved to be too much for Pope's Union army. By executing a flanking movement against the Union's left, Lee was able to achieve what Pope had been unable to do on the previous day. Many Northerners broke ranks and ran, and while Pope might later claim it to be an orderly retreat, it had most of the aspects of a rout. Still, again attesting to Renc's masterful leadership, his troops did not bolt. As the Union defeat became painfully apparent at dusk, a furious General Kearny rode up to Major General John Gibbon and said, "Reno is not stampeded, I am not stampeded, you are not stampeded. That is about all sir, my God, that's about all!"[13] As one of his last acts at Bull Run, Pope directed Reno and his men to move farther south along the battle line and serve as a rear guard to allow the rest of the Union army to escape eastward.[14] With aplomb, Reno carried out this order as directed, but, the day was Robert E. Lee's. His was the victory, and Jesse Reno was on the losing side.

Years later, in the flowery rhetoric of the 1880's, Brigadier General Orlando B. Willcox described Reno during the final action at Bull Run:

Look upon the picture, I pray of you, for a moment. A man shorter than Grant, about the height of Sheridan [5'5"], with whom he was most comparable in stature and equally unpretending, quietly sitting on horseback on the hill around which the battle rages. The last rays of the sun shines upon his calm, determined face. Nothing but the flash of his eye and a few sharp phrases falling from his lips denote the man of action and concentration of force. Right and left troops are giving away and batteries limbering up and fleeing, by him unnoticed, his attention fixed upon his own command. The enemy is surging over the field like waves of the sea, yet Reno sits like a rock, and there the proud waves are stayed.[15]

The bombastic and sometimes overconfident John Pope was blamed for the Northern defeat at Second Bull Run. He, in turn, blamed others, and not totally without cause. Fitz-John Porter, perhaps erroneously, was faulted for not attacking Jackson's flank. Pope was almost as vitriolic in his accusations of McClellan and some of the clique considered to be "McClellan's men". The rivalry of the egotistical McClellan and Pope certainly did little to help the Union cause. McClellan's jealous dislike of Pope was clearly reflected in several of his communications during the campaign. On August 28, Pope sent a request to Washington for more ammunition. McClellan's response was: "I know nothing of the calibres of Pope's artillery". Additionally, while Pope was deeply engaged in battle, McClellan is reported to have sent a communication to the administration in Washington, suggesting that it would be best "to leave Pope to get out of his scrape, and at once use all our means to make the capital perfectly safe." President Lincoln is said to have been aghast when he read the dispatch.

In light of these attitudes, it is not unexpected that many of McClellan's officers and cronies gave Pope less than full support.[16] Reno was, in every sense, an exception to that unfortunate and costly pettiness. He had just about all of the qualifications of a "McClellan man", having gone to school with McClellan, served under McClellan, and most importantly, received his generalcy through actions of McClellan. Yet, when it was all over, his character and professionalism left him untainted by the bitter feuding. General Pope later paid tribute to his faithful subordinate:

> I shall not soon forget the bright and confident face and the alert and hearty manner of that most accomplished and loyal soldier, General J. L. Reno. From first to last in this campaign he was always cheerful and ready, anxious to anticipate if possible, and prompt to execute with all his might, the orders he received. He was short in stature and upright in person, and with a face and manner so bright and encouraging at all times, but most especially noticeable in the fury of battle, that it was both a pleasure and a comfort to see him.[17]

9 — THE BATTLE AT CHANTILLY

There can be little doubt that Second Bull Run was an overwhelming victory for Robert E. Lee. Still, it was not the complete victory that Lee had desired—the destruction of Major General John Pope's Federal army. Following Pope's orders, Jesse Reno's corps provided rear guard allowing the rest of the Union army to escape eastward and take refuge in the old but formidable Confederate earthworks at Centreville, Virginia. Going east on the Warrenton Pike from Bull Run, the Union troops crossed over Cub Run and then traversed the long slope up to the heights of Centreville. Even though the Northern men were tired and beaten, Lee could readily determine that a frontal attack on Centreville could be at an unacceptable cost. Not to be stopped in his pursuit of Pope, however, Lee devised a new plan, and, had it been effective, might well have resulted in the capture of Washington and the fall of the Union.[1] The two West Point friends and classmates, Tom Jackson and Jesse Reno, would be key players in the coming events.

Lee's strategy appears to have embraced the philosophy that if you have a plan that works, stick with it. Jackson's flanking movement along the Rappahannock had been an outstanding success; why not try it again? If Jackson could circle around the Union line and come in on its rear, he could cut off Pope's retreat to the forts around Washington and possibly annihilate him. The plan was a sound one, and it might well have worked, were it not for several factors, including the fatigue of Lee's men, harsh weather and an unexpected Union reaction. About twenty miles east of Centreville is the town of Fairfax (then known as Fairfax Court House). On its western extremity, at a community then called Germantown, two major highways come together. The Warrenton Turnpike (now Route 29/211) comes in from the southwest to join the Little River Turnpike (Route 50). The basic ingredient of Lee's plan was to send Jackson (to be followed shortly thereafter by most of Longstreet's troops) almost straight north from the the the Bull Run battlefield. Coming to the Little River Turnpike, he would then move southeast following it to interdict Pope's escape route at Germantown.

On August 30, Pope's army had retreated to the area around Centreville. Meanwhile, a large but tardy body of Federal troops, dispatched from Alexandria, were about to reenforce Pope. In numbers, Pope would soon be stronger than his adversary. The poor morale of a large portion of his troops, however, precluded any attempt at a counterattack.

Reno and his 2nd Division of the IX Corps bivouacked on the east bank of Cub Run, two miles west of Centreville, where he was soon joined by Major General Isaac Stevens' 1st Division.[2] With his command reunited, Reno and his men could hope for a period of rest and recuperation. Reno, personally, appears to have been in particular need of a respite from his demanding command functions, for he is reported to have been suffering from an unspecified ailment. This sickness would affect him for the next several days.

Stonewall Jackson and his Southerners would have an even shorter respite than Reno. Tired and hungry at noon on August 31, they marched north through rain and mud, along country roads, in order to reach the Little River Turnpike. Turning southeast, they continued on for three and a half more miles to Pleasant Valley. There, with supply wagons far behind, they collapsed, wet, fatigued and hungry, and fell asleep beside the road.[3]

On August 31, 1862, Jackson's men were not the only units moving in northern Virginia. Federal wagon trains were rolling east on the Warrenton Pike and fresh Union troops were moving west to reenforce Pope. Lee also sent out cavalry to reconnoiter in advance of Jackson. The southern cavalry was under the command of Major General J. E. B. Stuart, and his mission was to unobtrusively gain intelligence relative to Union troop positions and movements. On nearing the Warrenton Turnpike during the evening, Stuart became aware of the heavy movement of wagons on the pike. Having a section of artillery with him, he could not resist firing six shots at the Union supply train. This attack served only as a detriment to Lee's well-laid plans. With his ineffective little artillery barrage, Stuart had alerted the Federal command to the threat of the planned attack. In most maneuvers of this sort, much of the success is dependent on the element of surprise. "Jeb" Stuart had given away any surprise that might have aided Jackson's attack the next day. General Pope heavily reinforced Fairfax Station and Germantown, with Major General Joseph Hooker in command of that area.[4]

The morning of September 1, 1862, was cold and blustery but, for the time, the rain had ceased. Jackson's men, still cold, hungry and weary, started plodding down the Little River Turnpike. Without their usual alacrity, they had travelled only five miles by about four o'clock that afternoon. Meanwhile, Pope had become aroused to the danger and, about 2:00 P.M., had dispatched Reno's two divisions to try to intercept Jackson on the Little River Turnpike. Although he accompanied his troops, Reno was still sick and placed operational command of the IX Corps in the capable hands of Major General Isaac Stevens. When the battle was actually joined, Reno remained on the field to assist in the placement of the various units.[5] Stevens rushed eastward on the Warrenton Pike and about a mile and a half from Germantown, turned north on a country road that intercepted the Little River Turnpike near Ox Hill and Chantilly (present day Pender). Coming suddenly into sight of Jackson's Confederates, the brilliant Stevens quickly assessed the situation and ordered his men to charge the enemy—an attack that came directly against the Confederate right flank. Jackson, the master of flanking movements, had been taken by his own game! Although his men outnumbered Reno's corps by more than two to one, Jackson's troops were surprised, confused and were halted about two miles from Germantown.

Jackson, faced with a potential enemy to his front, Hooker at Germantown, could ill afford to swing all of his own force away from that threat to cope with the attack on his flank. Stevens kept up pressure on Jackson's line and, as more Union troops arrived, Reno put them into position to support Steven's tactics. Fighting was intense and the IX Corps was effectively driving the Southerners back into the woods from whence they had come. After fighting aggressively for half an hour, the Union line stalled. Stevens, in order to spur his men on, took up the colors of his old regiment, the 79th New York, and personally led a revitalized attack. The 79th surged forward, and with it the other Federal regiments followed suit. At about five o'clock in the evening, as they were nearing the woods concealing the Confederates, Stevens, still in the lead, was shot in the head and died instantly. The death of this outstanding officer was not only a great loss to the Union, but also had the immediate effect of slowing the IX Corps' attack. Within a few minutes, Jackson's men had taken over the role of the aggressor and Reno's men were falling back.

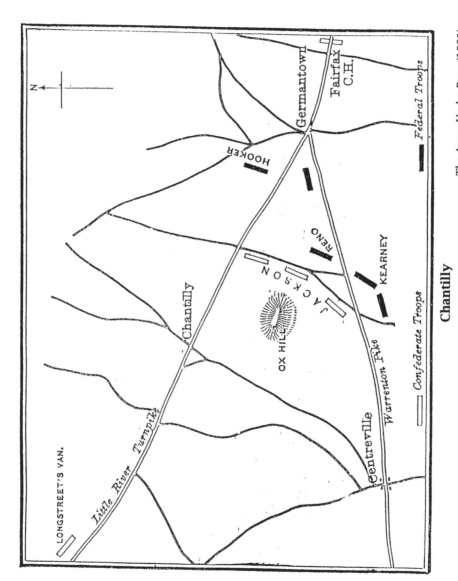

Chantilly

The Army Under Pope (1881)

At about the same time as Stevens' death, the weather also became a major participant in the fighting. A particularly hard and driving rainstorm commenced and continued until nightfall. The cloud-darkened sky, combined with the growing dusk of evening and gunsmoke, made enemy recognition a problem for both sides. The vicious rain also caused powder to become wet and foul many of the weapons. As a result, almost all semblance of organized combat degenerated into a melee, with muskets used as clubs in hand-to-hand struggle. Modern-day relic hunters have reported finding musket balls in some areas of the battlefield wherein 65% contained extraction holes. These corkscrew-like markings resulted from the necessity of removing the lead balls from the gun barrels, much in the same manner as one would remove a cork from a bottle. Their large numbers give an indication of the frequency of misfirings of the weapons due to wet powder.

Upon the death of General Stevens, Reno resumed command of the two IX Corps divisions.[7] At about the same time an aide of Stevens who had been sent to get reinforcements, reached Major General Philip Kearny on the Warrenton Pike. Kearny, who commanded the 1st Division of the III Corps, agreed to come to the aid of the embattled IX Corps. He immediately dispatched his leading brigade, under Brigadier General D. B. Birney, to report to Reno or Stevens. When Birney reached the battle scene at about 5:30 p.m., Reno directed him to quickly relieve the battered regiments. As Kearney and the rest of his division came into the area, they took up positions on the battle line, and the frenzied fighting continued in the rain and to near darkness. In trying to reposition some of the units, the dashing Kearny misidentified a Confederate regiment as one of his own and rode into its midst. Recognizing too late that he was within Confederate lines, the ever-daring Kearny refused to surrender and turned to ride away. He was shot from his horse and died within moments at about 6:15 p.m.[8] With Kearny and Stevens' deaths, the United States had lost two of its finer military leaders in just over an hour. Following Kearny's death, Birney assumed command of Kearny's division and led one last desperate bayonet charge.[9]

The rain, daylight and the fighting ceased at about 6:30 in the evening. Tactically, the battle ended in a stalemate. Although the Union forces withdrew from the field during the night, leaving it to the enemy, Stevens', Reno's and Kearney's men could take credit for allowing the rest of the Federal army to pass unscathed back to the security of the Washington forts. The army was safe, the capital did not fall and the nation remained to fight another day.

It has been implied that Reno did not give the full measure of command guidance that he should have at the Battle of Chantilly.

Any examination of his prior career, including his battle participation in the War with Mexico, as well as the Civil War, should suffice to show that he was not prone to shirking his responsibility. That he had the good judgement to remove himself from command at a time when he felt he could not operate at full competency attests to his concern for his men and the mission at hand. The fact that his assignment—to intercept and hold off Jackson—was fully achieved, makes any argument on the matter rhetorical.

During the early hours of September 2, Reno received orders to fall back from Chantilly and to proceed to Alexandria, Virginia, by way of the Little River Turnpike. Once at Alexandria, Reno was to report his position to Major General McClellan.[10] After carrying out these orders and departing Chantilly at 3:00 a.m., Reno advised McClellan later in the day that he was within three miles of Alexandria. He further stated that, "All of our wounded were placed in a hospital near the field."[11] Reno would find out the next day that he was in error in the latter statement. Out of concern for his men, he sent the following message:

Commanding Officer of Confederate Troops at or Near Chantilly:

Sir: I have just received information through Chaplain Ball of Twenty-first Massachusetts Volunteers, that about 250 of our wounded are now lying upon the battle-field of the 1st instant entirely destitute of medical attendance and provisions. I therefore respectfully request your permission to send forward, under flag of truce, Chaplain Ball and the medical director of this command, with the necessary medical stores and provisions for the comfort of these wounded, and to bring away such of them as are able to be removed[12]

This message appears to have been Reno's last significant action in support of Pope's Virginia campaign.

10 – THE ROAD TO FREDERICK

With his defeat in Virginia, Major General John Pope's star declined and he was soon banished to the West to campaign against Indians. Despite Pope's downfall, President Abraham Lincoln expressed empathy for him: "Pope did well, but there was an army prejudice against him, and it was necessary he should leave."[1] Once again Lincoln was faced with the dilemma of choosing a man to run the eastern army. Despite strong objections of most of his cabinet, Lincoln elected to put Major General George McClellan back in command, not only of his old army, but also of Pope's. Certainly Lincoln had no great fondness nor respect for McClellan, but he felt he had no other option. Ironically, this restoration to top level command would give McClellan his largest force ever, and would seem to be a promotion. About all this, the far from humble George McClellan wrote his wife: "Again I have been called upon to save the country."[2]

McClellan's promotion also increased Reno's status. With his new combined army, McClellan chose Burnside to lead a wing made up of two corps. This left the command of the entire IX Corps vacant and newly promoted (July 12, 1862) Major General Jesse Reno received the assignment. Instead of only twelve regiments as he had led at Bull Run, Reno had, on September 3, 1862, twenty-nine infantry regiments under his leadership, as well as sundry cavalry and artillery units.[3] He would not have to wait long to take his new command into battle.

The Confederates under Robert E. Lee had done well in Virginia, but the Federal capital still remained in Union hands and the Northern army was intact. Lee, wanting to stay on the offensive, needed a new plan of attack. Washington appeared to be too strongly defended for a direct attack, but Lee envisioned it being cut off from western support. For this reason, and others, he decided to invade the North by moving into Maryland. Conceptionally too, the only marginally pro-Union Marylanders might swing over to the South, once Lee and his men moved into the state. A successful invasion of the North might also get the Confederacy its much needed recognition and support from European countries. Such was the rationale of Robert E. Lee and Jefferson Davis on September 4, 1862, when the Confederate army crossed over the Potomac River thirty-five miles north of Washington, en route to Frederick, Maryland and other points north.[4]

IX Corps commander Reno also crossed the river and moved into Maryland on that same September 4. With his troops, Reno remained bivouacked at Meridan Hill near Rockville for about three days. McClellan received orders to send his army after Lee and, on the morning of September 7, elements of the IX Corps broke camp. They too headed north toward Frederick and by evening had marched about ten miles, encamping near the hamlet of Leesborough.[5] It was here, in the evening, that Reno had a momentous altercation with one of his regimental commanders—a future president of the United States.

In preparing for camping along the road, some of the men of the 23rd Ohio Volunteer Infantry Regiment were foraging hay for their horses from a stack in the adjoining field. Other reports indicated that the object of the foraging was either straw or grain. In any case, Reno had suddenly galloped up and observed the Ohio men in the act of pilfering. In Virginia and elsewhere in enemy territory, such action would have been termed "foraging". In friendly terrain, it was called stealing. Reno, described as irate over this indignity to Marylanders, addressed the Ohio men as: "You damned black sons of bitches", and demanded to talk to their colonel. Their colonel (actually lieutenant colonel) was Rutherford B. Hayes. Reno asked Hayes for his name, and Hayes told him. Then, knowing full well with whom he was speaking, Hayes impudently asked for Reno's name. After rebuking Hayes for a time, Reno's ire seemed to have subsided a bit and he told Hayes that they were in a loyal state and that he would not tolerate pilfering. Hayes, not above being snide, retorted: "Well, I trust our generals will exhibit the same energy in dealing with our foes that they do in the treatment of their friends." Reno was naturally offended and described as being "cut to the quick" by Hayes' remark. As he rode away his anger was further aggravated by the cheers of Hayes' men for their regimental commander. Later, Reno was said to have threatened to have Hayes put in irons.[6]

The impropriety of Reno's ill-chosen words to his subordinates is of course apparent. One should, however, consider his anger of the moment and the fact that military commanders are not generally known for graciously addressing errant troops. As for Reno's profanity, it may be noted that future president Rutherford Hayes, while giving a battle yell to his troops at South Mountain, yelled: "....Give the sons of bitches Hell."[7]

Military men, today, would be appalled at Hayes' impertinence in speaking as he had to such a high-ranking officer. More significantly, they might wonder how he got by with his insolence. Put into the context of the time however, the incident would seem a bit less shocking when considering the relative position of the state volunteer officer to the regular officer. The Reno-Hayes' confrontation was, to a degree, typical of the struggle between regular and volunteer officers throughout the war. The citizen-officer, more often than not, was appointed to his position because he was a local notable. In military service, he was often revered by his men because "he was one of them", and out to serve their purposes. The regular officer was in a minority and lacked such regional ties and the allegiance that might be derived thereof. Politics, too, was an important factor, and Hayes obviously fell into that category. By the beginning of the war, Rutherford Hayes was already more than a budding politician. Of his run-in with Reno, he seemed to have no great fear. On the day following the event, Hayes wrote to his uncle that: "...I have no doubt in any event that Governor [Salmon P.] Chase and the President will see justice done at the end to all our Ohio men."[8]

If Reno had any initial intention of pursuing the incident to the extent of court-martialing Hayes, he obviously dismissed the idea for, a full week later, no charges had been made. Whether Reno dismissed the thought of his own volition, or whether he took advice to do so, can only be speculated. It is known that Colonel Eliakim P. Scammon, Hayes' immediate superior, visited Reno in his quarters that night with the intent of easing the situation and erasing the ill feeling Reno might have toward Hayes. Scammon had been an instructor of Reno's when the latter was a cadet at West Point, and by way of a warning to his old student told him: "That the commander of the 23rd [Hayes] was something more than Lieut. Colonel of a regiment and it was always unwise to make enemies of such men or among the troops of their command." Although Scammon's admonition may have influenced Reno's decision to drop the issue, one other powerful political consideration must be viewed. Reno's commander and benefactor, George McClellan, had been appointed to his rank of major general by the governor of Ohio.[9]

For whatever his reason or reasons, Reno, a week later had apparently dropped any thought of taking disciplinary action against Hayes. On the battlefield at South Mountain, after Hayes had been seriously wounded and carried away, Reno came personally to bestow his praise on the 23rd Ohio. Years later Hayes wrote: "I was told while I was lying wounded that General Reno was greatly pleased by our vigorous attack, and that he had paid us high compliment, expressing gratification that our difficulty had gone no further than it did."[10] One might hope that this was the close of the unfortunate incident but, unfortunately, it was not. In a newspaper item, years after the war, a highly improbable claim was made that Reno was intentionally shot by a soldier of the 23rd Ohio to prevent a court-martialing of Hayes.[11] This unlikely circumstance will be discussed in a later chapter.

The remainder of the IX Corps' march to Frederick was leisurely and, for the most part uneventful. Reno, however, had one more disciplinary problem as his men entered the town. One of his brigades decided to put on a little show for the local populace by going through a drill routine. This bit of exhibitionism naturally slowed the progress of the remaining column of troops and was not to be tolerated by their resolute corps commander. Reno rode to the scene and firmly prodded the men to move along.[12]

On the evening of September 12, much of the IX Corps camped near Frederick. Reno and a part of the corps were already in the city and he would spend the night and most of the next morning as a guest at the Schley home on East Patrick Street. During that brief period he likely used the house as his headquarters.[13] Also, while in Frederick, there occurred an event that would entwine his name with one of the more enduring legends of the Civil War. Once again Jesse Reno and his old friend Stonewall Jackson were the leading players in a part fiction, part fact drama.

Only two days earlier, Jackson's Confederates had departed from Frederick and at that point, the famous story began. As legend has it, a little old lady in her nineties and fervently loyal to the Union, leaned from her dormer window and waved the Stars and Stripes in the face of the Southerners. Her name was Barbara Fritchie and she would become famous through a poem by John Greenleaf Whittier. Again, according to the legend, when she waved the flag some Confederate soldiers aimed their muskets at her and this inspired Whittier's lines:

"Shoot if you must this old grey head
But spare your country's flag," she said.

The Fritchie-Jackson story seems apocryphal at best, and its accuracy has been debated since its inception. Factual or not, Whittier's 30-couplet poem was an enormous success in the North

Roger Reno, Attorney

Reno family genealogist and distant relative of General Reno, standing beside the famous Barbara Fritchie flag which was used to cover Jesse Reno's coffin. The flag was temporarily brought to the South Mountain area for the one-hundredth anniversary celebration of the erection of the Reno monument.

"... Shoot if you must this old grey head but spare your country's flag," she said.

and it spread like wildfire. Many historical accounts now question whether the event ever occurred.

Much better substantiated is Reno's reported meeting with the same lady as he was leaving Frederick on September 13.[14] With his brother Frank and part of his staff, Reno was riding along Patrick Street, when he observed a gathering of people in front of the widow Fritchie's house. He stopped, was invited in and accepted her offer of a glass of her homemade currant wine. Upon his departure, Mrs. Fritchie took down a large bunting flag from her dormer window and presented it to the general. As Reno left he handed the flag to his brother and remarked: "Frank, whom does she [Barbara Fritchie] put you in mind of?" Frank replied "Mother", and Reno nodded his head in affirmation. Frank Reno folded the flag and put it in his saddlebag. Jesse Reno rode off to his destiny—his death the following day. The Barbara Fritchie flag would cover his casket at his funeral.[15]

11 – TOUCHED BY FATE

Since assuming command of the Army of Northern Virginia, Confederate General Robert E. Lee had achieved much success in the fighting in Virginia. The capture of the Federal capital had eluded him, however, and as mentioned in the previous chapter, he made the decision to press the attack and invade the North by way of Maryland. If successful in this venture, he hoped to see Maryland swing over to the side of the South. Further, he considered that battle successes in the North might bring the Confederacy the support it greatly needed from European countries, particularly France and England. Thus, Lee moved his troops into the North by way of Frederick, Maryland.

After leaving Frederick, Lee led his army over the mountains to the west and set up his headquarters near Boonsboro. At this point, he determined his next objective to be the capture of the Federal arsenal at Harpers Ferry. If allowed to continue, that garrison could be a thorn in his side for it held the potential of interdicting his supply line to the South. Lee, with Major General Thomas J. (Stonewall) Jackson's assistance, conceived of a three-pronged attack on Harpers Ferry. It required more than half of Lee's army and would spread his force over a relatively wide area. Lee's other senior deputy, Major General James Longstreet, opposed the risky venture but, as a soldier, abided by his orders.[1] Lee again was relying on the dilatory Major General George McClellan to aid him in carrying out the plan. To some degree, McClellan surprised Lee by moving faster than expected, but not fast or deftly enough to avoid the loss of Harpers Ferry.

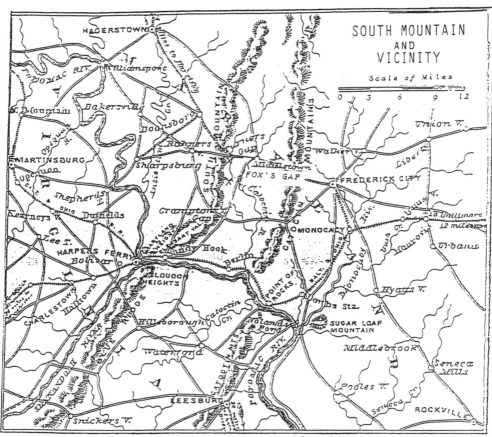

*Adapted from History of the Civil War
in America, Vol. II (1866)*

   Lee's risky plan worked and the threat posed by Harpers Ferry
was eliminated, but, despite its accomplishment, his Maryland campaign failed. On September 13, a bizarre event, one of the more
momentous twists of fate of the Civil War, occurred and had tremendous ramifications. Because of it, battles would be fought at
South Mountain and Antietam, Lee's Maryland campaign would be
a failure, and ultimately it contributed to the South's defeat.
   Corporal Barton W. Mitchell, Company F, 27th Indiana Volunteers, in another time, might have gone down in history as a hero
because of his fortuitous discovery and prompt action. To his misfortune, however, he died about 3 1/2 years later, unheralded and in
poverty. On Saturday morning, September 13, 1862, the 27th Indiana set up camp in a meadow near Frederick which recently had
been vacated by Confederate troops. The observant Corporal Mitchell

spied three cigars wrapped with a piece of paper laying on the ground. The writing on the paper included the names of several prominent Confederate generals and Mitchell was astute enough to realize that he had in his hands something of possible significance. Indeed he did have, for the paper was Lee's operational order to his commanders, detailing their assigned actions and locations. Special Order No. 191 became famous as the "Lost Order".[2] Little time was spent in getting the important document into proper channels, and by noon McClellan could revel in his great fortune in knowing his opponent's plans. With elation, he told one of his generals, "Here is a paper with which if I cannot whip Bobby Lee, I will be willing to go home."[3] The "Lost Order" was, in fact, the means by which McClellan could make good his claim. However, "Little Mac" was a creature of habit and speedy action was not his way. As he had done frequently in the past, he grossly overestimated his enemy's strength, claiming it greatly outnumbered his. This also added to his caution. He estimated Lee's force to number 120,000, when, in fact, it was considerably less than half that amount. McClellan's strength was about 87,000 men.[4] As succeeding events proved, McClellan again dallied too long to realize the full benefits that the "Lost Order" offered him.

On September 13, rather than taking immediate and all-out action against the widely separated elements of Lee's army, McClellan wasted most of the day and let his fortuitous advantage slip through his fingers. Had he moved at that time, he could have likely crossed South Mountain with little opposition other than that provided by Confederate cavalry led by Major General James E. B. Stuart. Lee's small remaining force at Boonsboro would have been easy prey and the other parts of his army would have also been at great disadvantage. Instead of moving his entire army, as he should have, McClellan merely dispatched his own cavalry, under Brigadier General Alfred Pleasonton, westward to clear the Catoctin Mountain Range and South Mountain of any enemies that might hinder his later passage to Boonsboro. Additionally, McClellan sent Major General Jesse Reno and three of the four divisions of Reno's IX Corps ten miles west to Middletown to support Pleasonton, should he need infantry assistance. At this point, and apparently well into the morning of September 14, there is no indication that McClellan had any idea that he would be fighting a battle at South Mountain, or that he had formulated any overall plans for his army to engage the enemy there.

McClellan might well have gotten away with his unhurried action and succeeded in his plan to trap Lee had not another fateful circumstance occurred. In Frederick, at the time of McClellan's elation over his good fortune of possessing the "Lost Order", a civilian

Southern sympathizer was, for unrecorded reasons, present at McClellan's headquarters. Unsubstantiated legend has it that this man became aware of the fact that McClellan possessed Lee's fateful order. More realistically, he was perhaps alerted by the westward movements of Pleasonton and Reno's troops. Whichever the case, this diligent adherent to the rebel cause located and passed his information to J. E. B. Stuart. Stuart, in turn, sent the critical information on to Lee. On receiving the word of his precarious situation at about 10 p.m. on the night of September 13, Lee immediately reacted by dispatching Major General Daniel H. Hill with two infantry brigades and a battery of artillery to make a stand and hold the gaps at South Mountain. Hill's meager force also included Stuart's cavalry regiment. Further, Longstreet's command, then at Hagerstown, was ordered to start marching at the next dawn and come to Hill's support. Lee also directed Jackson to expedite his efforts at Harpers Ferry in order that the Confederate army could be reunited as soon as possible.[5] Thus, unknown to McClellan, Lee had taken action which would lead to a battle at South Mountain.

As mentioned, Reno and three divisions of his corps were given orders to move from Frederick to Middletown on September 13. Major General Ambrose Burnside travelled with them.[6] They departed Frederick around 2 p.m. and spent the night near the foot of South Mountain, camped around Middletown. Whether Reno had time then, or during the following morning, to enjoy the wild beauty of the mountains and reflect on his youth in similarly timbered hills around Franklin, Pennsylvania, can only be surmised. The eastern slope of South Mountain then, as now, was sparsely populated and had only an occasional clearing for fields among the densely timbered hills. In many areas of Fox's Gap, the undergrowth is a wild tangle of vines, making passage difficult. Mid-September, in many years, can bring a tinge of color to the trees and bushes, adding to the spectacle of beautiful vistas throughout the hills. Enjoying the cool evening in that natural splendor Reno, like McClellan, probably sensed no ominous foreboding of a battle the next day in these lush hills.

On Sunday morning, Pleasonton's cavalry soon encountered stiff enemy opposition in the middle of one of the gaps crossing South Mountain, Fox's Gap. He immediately requested infantry support and Reno, at 6 a.m., sent his Fourth Division (known as the Kanawha Division) forward to engage and clear the rebels from the pass. The six infantry regiments of this division were manned entirely by Ohio volunteers and were under the command of Brigadier General Jacob D. Cox. Prior to engaging the Confederates at about 9 a.m., Cox had become alerted to the fairly heavy concentration of enemy troops ahead of him and had passed the word on to Reno. At this point, around

8 a.m., Reno advised that he would send the rest of the IX Corps to assist Cox.[7] For whatever reason or reasons, Reno did not carry out that promise with his usual promptness. Whether he had become infected with a bit of McClellan's propensity for dallying, or had been restrained from taking quick action by his superiors is not recorded. His nearest other division, under Brigadier General Orlando Willcox, did not depart their camp at Middletown until about 10:30 a.m. and, because of an error in routing, did not reach Cox and the battle zone until two in the afternoon.[8] This was during a lull in the fighting and well after the hectic battle Cox had had with the Confederates during most of the morning. Starting about 9 a.m., the church bells of Middletown were interrupted with the sound of cannon and musket to the west. Cox's Ohioans had fought valiantly in charging up the mountain and, during the viciously contested action, Lieutenant Colonel Rutherford Hayes was badly wounded in the arm.

Reno's last two divisions were even later in reaching Fox's Gap for they had farther to travel. They were additionally delayed by Reno's superior, General Burnside, who directed that they not go into battle until their action could be coordinated with Major General Joseph Hooker's to the north at Turner's Gap.[9] Burnside's intercession here may provide a hint to the cause of Reno's slow action in the morning.

By 3:30 or 4 p.m. Reno's entire IX Corps had arrived on the battle line and he went to Fox's Gap to personally direct his command. The fighting, which had started again about 2 p.m., continued intermittently until near sundown.[10] While the Union line had been greatly augmented with Reno's remaining divisions during the mid-afternoon, the Confederates had been given grace time to also bring up reserves in the form of Longstreet's nine brigades.[11] Word was finally given, at 4 p.m., for the entire Union line to move forward and drive the enemy from Fox's and Turner's Gaps.

Progress was made on both the left and center of the Federal line, but due to the steep and rough terrain on the right side of Reno's troops, the attack was stalled. At about 6 p.m., he rode forward with his staff to determine what might be delaying the right side movement.[12] Rather than going directly to his right flank, however, General Reno rode to the left flank so that he might move along the entire line of regiments and compliment them on their excellent progress and battle conduct. While on the left and congratulating Colonel Eliakim Scammon, who commanded a brigade that included Rutherford Hayes' regiment, Reno conveyed high praise on the Ohioans for their performance. He also expressed gratitude that his earlier difficulty with Hayes had gone no further than it did.

Scammon was impressed with the indication that Reno wished to sooth any irritation the incident may have caused.[13]

Leaving Scammon, Reno continued riding northward along the regimental fronts, congratulating each as he progressed along the line. Accounts of various historians and observers differ somewhat concerning what actually happened next, but the essence of their chronicles is generally in accord. Reno had gone halfway or more along the line when, still to the front of the Union forces and in an exposed position, he turned toward the enemy's position to make observations with a telescope. The lack of enemy firing for a time gave the misleading impression that the Confederates had permanently vacated their line behind stone walls. Suddenly musket fire erupted from the front. Confusion spread among Union regiments, some of which where fresh in battle and were at that time being moved to the front. During this time, Reno was struck by a bullet, which, by some accounts, hit the spine and lodged in his chest. Carried a short distance to the rear, Reno saw his old friend and classmate, Brigadier General Samuel D. Sturgis, and called out, "Hallo Sam, I'm dead!" Sturgis, at first thought Reno was joking and replied, "Oh no, General, not so bad as that I hope." But Reno added: "Yes, yes, I'm dead—good-bye!"[14]

Reno was carried back down the mountain, about three-quarters of a mile from where he fell, placed under a large oak tree along the road and cared for by his surgeon, Dr. Calvin Cutter.[15] About 7 p.m., Jesse Lee Reno, age thirty-nine, passed into eternity. Shortly

Wise's field, site of fatal wounding of General Reno.

The Reno Oak
Site of General Reno's Death

The Valley Register

before the end, he said, "Tell my command that if not in body I will be with them in spirit."[16]

His old friend Ambrose Burnside issued the following official announcement of Reno's death:

General Orders,   Headquarters Ninth Army Corps,
    No. 17   Mouth Antietam, Md., September 20, 1862

The commanding general announces to the corps the loss of their late leader, Maj. Gen. Jesse L. Reno.

By the death of this distinguished officer the country loses one of its most devoted patriots, the army one of its most thorough soldiers. In the long list of battles in which General Reno has fought in his country's service, his name always appears with the brightest luster, and he has now bravely met a soldier's death while gallantly leading his men at the Battle of South Mountain.

For his high character and the kindly qualities of his heart in private life, as well as for the military genius and personal daring which marked him as a soldier, his loss will be deplored by all who knew him, and the commanding gen-

eral desires to add the tribute of a friend to the public mourn-
ing for the death of one of the country's best defenders.

By command of Major-General Burnside.[17]

Almost from the time of his death, there has been considerable speculation as to whose bullet, friend's or foe's, caused the
mortal wounding of Jesse Reno. A preponderance of published accounts holds with the notion that he was hit by a Confederate musket ball; but there has been a persistent belief by some that he was
accidentally struck by a bullet fired by one of his own men. The
passage of more than a century has not served to positively answer
the question and, unless new evidence is brought forward, it is doubtful that it will ever be absolutely resolved. Even General Orlando
Willcox, speaking at the dedication of the Reno monument on South
Mountain twenty-seven years later, skirted the issue by saying that
Reno was hit "by a sharpshooter—possibly a stray bullet."[18] There
has even been a ludicrous claim that Reno was intentionally shot by
an Ohio soldier to prevent him from court-martialing Rutherford
Hayes. When fact and legend blend over a long period and opposing
sides have arisen, it is difficult to sway adherents from their respective positions. It is, therefore, not the intent herein to provide a
definitive position on that fateful event, but rather, to present various circumstances and observations that indicate what most likely
happened. The three suggested causes of Reno's death, as mentioned above, will be examined in order, starting with the least prob-
able: that he was intentionally killed by one of his own men.

The basis for the story that Reno was willfully killed appears
to have stemmed from a footnote published in an 1882 history of
the 21st Regiment of Massachusetts Volunteers:

> General Reno took Lieutenant-Colonel Hayes severely
> though justly to task, in the presence of his men, for their
> piratical conduct, shortly before the battle of South Moun-
> tain; and some scribbler in a communication published in
> the Boston Journal some years ago writes that a member of
> the 23rd Ohio murdered General Reno in that battle to pre-
> vent the general from court-martialing his lieutenant-colo-
> nel for allowing such misconduct. I need not say to any one
> familiar with the circumstances of General Reno's death that
> he was not so killed.[19]

While the above report could give rise to spectacular headlines,
such as: General Murdered To Protect Future President, virtually no
credence can be given to its occurrence. The 23rd Ohio was positioned very near the left flank of the entire Union line and, after
visiting it, Reno had moved up the line, passing several other regiments. The frontage of a regiment is approximately 277 yards, while

the effective killing range of a single rifled-musket shot was only about 250 yards.[20] A military map showing evening positions of Union forces, indicates that the 23rd Ohio was about 900 yards from Reno when he was shot.[21] To make such a shot at dusk, over rolling terrain with intervening stone walls and undergrowth and at a man mounted on horseback, would be miraculous, if not impossible. Moreover, Colonel Scammon, brigade commander, who had shortly before been with Reno, stated that they were talking just at the right rear of the 23rd, and that Reno rode off along the crest of the hill "until concealed by a clump of trees".[22] Thus, Reno would not even have been visible to the men of the 23rd Ohio.

Those theorizing that Reno was shot accidentally by one of his own men do have some substantive and supportive circumstances to argue their case. However, factual data falls far short of that needed to confirm what actually happened at that fateful time. Several accounts indicate that there had been a lull in Confederate shooting opposite the IX Corps position and some commanders had taken advantage of the respite to replace spent units in the front line with fresh regiments which had been held in reserve. Some of the replacement units were green and totally inexperienced in battle and, while moving forward, were unexpectedly fired upon from frontal areas thought to have been vacated by the enemy. In the confusion that followed, some Union units were actually firing in the direction of friendly troops.[23] At about that same time, Reno was in an extremely advanced and exposed position and, conceivably, could have been hit by the indiscriminate shooting.

Perhaps significantly contributing to the "shot by own men" theory, is a statement attributed to Jesse Reno himself, in which he, after being wounded, reportedly told one of his generals, "...I am killed. Shot by our own men."[24] Reno was probably basing his observation on the mistaken belief that there were no enemy in his immediate front. His purported statement may have impressed those within hearing, and persisted in related accounts in subsequent years. Other accounts support the fact that, shortly after Union reconnaissance had reported no enemy in the area, Confederate troops had reoccupied the woods opposite the site of Reno's wounding, and further, that they had opened fire from that position.[25]

Another factor, possibly contributing to the idea that Reno was accidentally shot, is the romanticist's comparison of the lives of Jesse Reno and Thomas Stonewall Jackson. They both were from West Virginia; they were friends at the military academy; they fought each other in two Civil War battles; both were linked with the famous Barbara Fritchie flag; Jackson had a "Stonewall Brigade"; Reno had a "Stonewall Regiment"; Thomas Jonathan Jackson was accidentally and fatally shot by his own men—so why not Jesse Lee Reno? Such are the elements of lasting legends.

Recollections of old soldiers also add to the lore of battles. All too frequently, however, their accounts are incorrect and tainted with embellishments and faulty remembrances. The "I was there, I should know" comments often fail to relate actual events. During the early 1880's there was a flurry of veterans' letters published in the *National Tribune* (a military journal of that time) relative to the circumstances of Reno's death. One letter, in particular, was emphatic in its proclamation that Jesse Reno was, in fact, killed by one of his own men. Published on July 26, 1883, a Sergeant A. H. Wood claimed to have been an orderly for Reno and to have had detailed information concerning the general's death. In Wood's account, he does not claim to be an actual witness to the shooting but rather, seems to be recounting what he says a fellow orderly, Martin Fecken, observed. At, or just before the time of the shooting, Wood stated that he, himself, had ridden forward and had not observed any enemy troops to his front. Other essential elements of Wood's story follow. Reno had ridden forward, accompanied only by his staff surgeon and one other orderly. While Reno was at that location, according to Wood, "...a soldier suddenly wheeled around and with the exclamation of 'Rebel cavalry!' aimed his musket at them. In vain the orderly cried out: 'Don't fire!' The man discharged his piece, and the ball struck Reno in the lower part of the chest." Wood asserted that the guilty party was a member of the 20th Michigan or from Edward Ferrero's brigade. Further in his letter, Wood stated that the orderlies were ordered by members of Reno's staff to say nothing about the shooting and to keep quiet. He said he abided by the order for twenty years, but no longer felt compelled to do so.[26]

Sergeant Wood's story cannot be totally discounted but certainly some of his statements merit critical examination. It is worth noting that the subsequent published responses of five other men all contested Wood's account.[27] The claim that Reno's escort consisted only of his surgeon and one orderly seems highly improbable. One might think that the least likely staff person the general would take with him on a reconnoitering trip would be his surgeon. Since the battle had been going on all day, it could be assumed that the doctor would be more appropriately occupied tending the wounded. In fact, in his post-battle report, General Edward Ferrero wrote that: "Dr. Calvin Cutter, brigade surgeon, although injured on the 13th by a blow from a horse, was unremitting in his attentions to the wounded, and was of invaluable service."[28] Another unusual aspect of Sergeant Wood's composition of Reno's escort, is that none of Reno's aides-de-camp were with him, as would be normal. This was despite the fact that, as a major general and corps commander, Reno then had four aides: his brother, Lieutenant B. F. Reno, and Lieutenants John A. Morris, T. B. Marsh, and Charles G. Hutton.[29]

The principal flaw in Sergeant Wood's account was the citing of the 20th Michigan. This unit was not a part of the IX Corps, nor was it even on the field of battle. Wood's assertion that Reno's orderlies were silenced, gives additional cause for doubt. What about the other men in the alleged shooter's unit—were they not close enough to hear the purported exclamations and observe the man's actions? Were they also silenced through the subsequent years? If Wood's story had real substance, one might expect that others would have come forward to give him support.

Strong support for the conviction that Reno was killed by an enemy bullet comes from the enemy itself. General D. H. Hill, commanding the Confederate forces at the Battle of South Mountain, officially reported, "The Yankees on their side lost General Reno, a renegade Virginian, who was killed by a happy shot from the Twenty-third North Carolina."[30] Confederate brigade commander Col. D. K. McRae also cited Reno's death in his official report. In discussing the actions of the 23rd North Carolina, McRae said, "It was by the fire of this regiment that General Reno was killed and a portion of his staff wounded, the fact having been reported to me at the time of its occurrence."[31] The most specific account of Reno's death by the Twenty-third North Carolina Regiment occurred in its unit history:

> General Jesse L. Reno, commanding the corps assailing us, and who had been prominent in the capture of Roanoke Island, Kinston, and other places in North Carolina, was killed at long range by Charles W. Bennett, of Granville County, Orderly Sergeant of Company E. Sergeant Bennett was severely wounded at Sharpsburg.[32]

Possibly the most believable account, and one supporting the concept that Reno was killed by enemy fire, comes from a letter written in 1899 by Captain Gabriel Campbell who had commanded Company E of the 17th Michigan Regiment at the battle. Campbell, at the time of the writing, was a professor at Dartmouth College in New Hampshire and was responding to a query about his recollections of the battle. His statements were sufficiently detailed and precise as to give credulity to his narrative. Campbell stated that during the lull in the fighting in the evening, he and a small detachment of men had gone forward, for the purpose of recovering the wounded, in the area where shortly Reno would be shot. Campbell was the last leaving the field but said that before his departure, rebel soldiers came out of the opposing woods and were pilfering from the dead on the field and picking up abandoned weapons.

Further, Campbell stated that a short time later he pointed out some of these rebel soldiers to General Willcox. Subsequently, Campbell said that he had met Reno quietly riding to the front with four or five members of his staff and there Reno peered through his field glass. Then, Campbell reported "...there was a sudden fusilade —five or six shots in about a couple of seconds. There was at once commotion among the Reno horsemen, a dismounting and a catching of someone. Evidently the rebels had begun to form behind the stone fence. Quickly an orderly comes back leading several horses. To my inquiry, 'what happened?' he answered, 'Reno is shot!' Immediately men bearing the General on a blanket follow. They pause as they meet me, and are glad of a little assistance in carrying the middle of the blanket on the right side, which duty fell to me." Later, in his letter, Campbell surmised that Reno's mistaken belief that there were no rebels to his immediate front, led to his stating that he had been shot by his own men.[33]

Again, it seems doubtful that the source of Jesse Reno's death will likely ever be conclusively resolved. An extract from one of his regiments' histories seems befitting of the circumstance: "During that fire, Reno fell, mortally wounded, and who can say what bullets pierced him—friend's or foe's? Ah! the little General was well loved— his loss was a great blow to the Ninth Corps; the bitterness would have been lessened but for the lingering doubt of his having been killed by rebel shots."[34]

12 – Our True And Loved Commander

Even in the terse and usually prosaic tone of official military reports, there sometimes slips in a hint of personal emotion and affection. Such was the case in Major General Ambrose Burnside's report after the Battle of South Mountain:

> I will not attempt in a public report to express the deep sorrow which the death of the gallant Reno caused me. A long and intimate knowledge of his high and noble character had endeared him to me, as well as to all with whom he had served. No more valuable life than his has been lost during this contest for our country's preservation.[1]

A number of regimental histories, written after the Civil War, eulogized Reno in a most respectful and often affectionate manner. The best representation of these was the one included in the history of the 21st Massachusetts Volunteer Regiment:

> ...our true and loved commander, General Jesse L. Reno, the soldier without spot or blemish, fell mortally wounded by a musket shot in the breast, and died in about an hour. We were on the right flank of his old brigade, and there was not a man in the 21st who did not love him, he had always stood with his men in battle, in a position to know the varying chances of the fight, and every man felt sure that his life would not be unnecessarily sacrificed when Reno was in command. The long, hard month on the "Northerner" had established confidential relations between General Reno and the regiment, such as have rarely existed between a general and

his men, he had daily shown his interest in the promotion of our comfort, and an eagerness to add to our military education and efficiency, and when we first met the enemy under him showed that he relied on us as we did on him.[2]

With these words of sincere affection, one can also remember Mary Reno's words when writing to her husband some years earlier, "The servants seem much distressed at your departure and I heard a good many sobs and groans after you left. I surely believe everyone loves you."

Major General George B. McClellan in his official report, briefly but with sincerity, wrote: "In General Reno the nation lost one of its best general officers. He was a skillful soldier, a brave and honest man."[3] Additionally, McClellan said of Reno, "The loss of this brave and distinguished officer tempered with sadness the exultations of triumph. A gallant soldier, an able general, endeared to his troops and associates, his death is felt as an irreparable misfortune."[4]

For those who might wish to draw comparison to the many coincidences that seemed to intertwine the lives of those two friends from West Point, Jesse Lee Reno and Thomas Jonathan Jackson, it can be some solace to know that Jackson and his men had nothing to do with Reno's death. Still, there was a tie between them, even on that sad occasion: Enemy troops claiming to have shot Reno were under the command of Major General Daniel Harvey Hill, Stonewall Jackson's brother-in-law.

After Jesse Reno's death, his brother Frank took his remains to Baltimore for embalming and viewing at the establishment of a Mr. Weaver. There, dressed in uniform, Reno was reportly viewed by a number of people on the morning of September 16. That afternoon the body was sent by rail to Boston, Massachusetts, where Mary Reno and her young sons were living. The Barbara Fritchie flag covered his coffin.[5] Possibly at Mary's request and with a desire to save Reno's uniform for the sons, it was reported that he was dressed in civilian clothes while at Baltimore.

His funeral was held at Trinity Church in Boston on Friday, September 19, and his body placed in a vault in the church with the intent of reintering it at some future date. Also, at the request of friends, there was no military display.[6] This doubtless reflected Mary Reno's wishes, but it can only be speculated as to her reason for this. She not only had lost her husband to war, but also her father some sixteen years earlier. Perhaps bitterness, coupled with a remembrance of the traumatic experience of her father's elaborate military funeral provided the basis for her decision. At his death, Jesse Reno was 39 years old and Mary was 34. She would not remarry. For many years, she kept the Barbara Fritchie flag, together with Reno's uniform and sword, in an army chest.[7]

Jesse Lee Reno's family is buried around him in Oak Hill Cemetery, Georgetown, Washington, D.C.

Louise McConnell

At the conclusion of the Civil War, Mary Reno returned to her home city of Washington, D.C. and purchased a large circular burial plot in the Oak Hill Cemetery in Georgetown. She chose a centrally

Reno Monument
South Mountain, Maryland

Timothy S. McConnell

**Dedication of the Reno Monument
South Mountain, Maryland
September 14, 1889**

The Valley Register

Reno Monument, South Mountain, 1989
Author speaking at the 100th anniversary rededication ceremony.

Louise McConnell

94

One hundredth anniversary rededication ceremony, Reno monument, in 1989.
As on the original occasion, the rain was heavy.

Louise McConnell

located knoll that commanded a view in all directions. On April 9, 1867, Jesse Reno was reintered at Oak Hill. A slender draped shaft of marble marks his resting place. Three days later, Mary Reno also had their three children, who had died in childhood, reintered there near their father. Mary Cross Reno died of "nervous prostration" on April 18, 1880, and two days later was laid beside her beloved Jesse. Ultimately, all five of Mary and Jesse's children were buried in the plot, as were also the wives of the two sons. Even with the nine burials on what is now known as Reno Circle, only a little over one-third of the plot has been utilized. Mary perhaps envisioned that she and Jesse would have grandchildren and other descendents. In this assumption she was wrong. Nevertheless, at Oak Hill Cemetery, Jesse Lee Reno is surrounded by gravestones bearing the names of many notables.

As indicated above, of Mary and Jesse's four sons and one daughter: Lewis, Marian (daughter), Alexander, Conrad and Jesse Wilford, only the last two would grow to adulthood. Both of these sons would reflect their father's brilliance and capability by achieving prominence in their own right. Both, for example, were to have biographical sketches in *Who's Who In America 1924-1925.*[8]

Conrad, born in 1859, was a prominent Boston lawyer for almost thirty years. He drafted a number of bills for Congress between 1907 and 1922 and was the author of several scholarly legal works. As was the case with his younger brother, Conrad was also an inventor. He is credited with inventing the "stream" method of wireless transmission of energy and a system for transmitting energy without wires. He also was the discoverer of the spirally revolving magnetic field. Married for 46 years to Susan Eustis, Conrad died childless at age 73 in 1933.[9] In his will, he left their father's sword to his younger brother, Jesse Wilford.

The youngest of Jesse Reno's children, Jesse Wilford, may have achieved the most fame of all. Born in 1861, he became a prominent engineer and inventor. In 1891 he perfected a plan for the construction of subways in New York City. Later he was to be known as "the man who saved New York City from the elevated." Jesse Wilford also had the distinction of being the first man to build an electric railroad in the South. He went on to invent other things, but in our present day society, we should likely honor him for inventing our energy saving device, the "inclined elevator" or escalator. Jesse Wilford married the widowed Baroness Marie G. Snowman in 1901. It was she who collected Reno family records. Unfortunately, since her death in 1955, these seem to have been lost or discarded. As was the case with his brother Conrad, Jesse Wilford sired no children. He died at 86 in 1947, and with him, the lineage of Jesse Lee Reno ceased.[10]

The Reno brothers were not solely dedicated to serious endeavors for they both enjoyed sports and it was they who brought the game of tennis to the United States. They later introduced Dwight F. Davis to the game, and to him we owe the Davis Cup competition.[11]

After Jesse Lee Reno's death, he was honored by having several military sites named after him. Two cities would also preserve his name, El Reno, Oklahoma and Reno, Nevada. The latter was given its name by Central Pacific Railroad officials in 1868.

On September 14, 1889, 27 years after he was killed, survivors of General Reno's IX Corps and others came back to the mountains of Maryland and to the site of his death. There they unveiled a monument to his memory. Although the weather was rainy and disagreeable, about a thousand people gathered for the ceremony. The orator for the occasion was Major General Orlando B. Willcox, who had commanded a division under Reno at the Battle of South Mountain.[12]

On the one hundredth anniversary of the monument's dedication, historians, devotees of Civil War studies and reenactors from Michigan, Virginia, Illinois, Nevada and Maryland gathered on the weekend of September 15-17, 1989, to once again recall what had happened on the mountain and to honor all who had fallen there. Under the sponsorship of the Middletown Valley Historical Society and the Frederick County Civil War Roundtable, in cooperation with Antietam National Park, the Reno monument was rededicated. Again, as in 1889, those wishing to honor Major General Jesse Lee Reno and his contributions to the preservation of his country, stood in the driving rain to "Remember Reno".

– *ENDNOTES*

CHAPTER ONE

1. Roger Reno, Rockford, Illinois, and William L. Reno, Falls Church, Va., extensive unpublished Reno family genealogical information.
2. Ibid.; *Encyclopedia of American Biography, New Series*, Vol. 21 (New York: American Historical Company, 1949), 94.
3. Alfred H. Guernsey and Henry M. Alden, *Harper's Pictorial History of the Civil War* (New York: Fairfax Press, reprint, n.d.), 398n.
4. History of Venango County, Pennsylvania, 1890. Reprint, Venango County Historical Society, Franklin, Pa., 1984, 361.
5. History of Venango County, Pennsylvania, 1879. Reprint, Venango County Historical Society, Franklin, Pa., 1976, 176.
6. Ibid.

CHAPTER TWO

1. Pauline Lillie, Marengo the County Seat - Marengo the Town (Marengo, Iowa 125th Celebration Committee,1984), 172-73.
2. Franklin, Pennsylvania, Public Library. Newspaper clipping file: "Reno".
3. Gen. C. H. Barney, *The Reno Memorial,* South Mountain, Md., (The Society of the Burnside Expedition and of the Ninth Army Corps, 1891), 12.
4. Frank N. Schubert, *Vanguard of Expansion* (Washington: Government Printing Office, 1980), 80-81.
5. George W. Cullum, *Biographical Register of the Officers and Graduates of the U.S. Military Academy* (Cambridge, Mass.: Riverside Press, 1891), 262.
6. Steven W. Sears, *Landscape Turned Red* (New York: Popular Library, 1985), 155.
7. George Walton, *Sentinel of the Plains: Fort Leavenworth and the American West* (New York: Prentice-Hall Inc., 1973), 120.
8. Barney, 12.
9. USMA Archives, Cadet Delinquency Record.

10. USMA Archives, Post Order Book #2, Special Orders 107 & 119.
11. USMA Archives, Cadet Delinquency Record.
12. Cullum, 262.

CHAPTER THREE

1. Russell F. Weigley, *History of the United States Army* (Bloomington: Indiana University Press, 1984), 185.
2. Ibid., 184–85.
3. Ibid., 169.
4. Cullum, *Biographical Register*, Vol. 2, 262.
5. Robert M. Utley, *Frontiersmen in Blue* (Lincoln: University of Nebraska Press, 1967), 2.
6. Weigley, 184.
7. Jesse Reno's notarized statement of Mexican War Service, October 31, 1850. Statement made for purpose of securing bounty land. Pension Records, National Archives.
8. *Universal Standard Encyclopedia*, Vol. 20 (New York: Standard Reference Works Publishing Co., Inc., 1958), 7262.
9. Frank H. Winter and Mitchell R. Sharp, "Major Lion's Rocketeers: The New York Rocket Battalion," *Civil War Times Illustrated*, Vol. 11, No. 9, January, 1973, 14.
10. Instruction for Mountain Howitzers, prepared by a board of army officers, 1851, (Washington: Gibbon & Co).
11. Edward D. Mansfield, *The Mexican War* (New York: A. S. Barnes & Co., 1858), 163-68.
12. Fairfax Downey and Paul Angle, *Texas and the War With Mexico* (New York: American Heritage Publishing Co. Inc., 1961), 71.
13. Mansfield, 167-68.
14. Ibid., 169.
15. Downey and Angle, 105–106.
16. Ibid.
17. Mansfield, 171.
18. K. Jack Bauer, *The Mexican War 1846-1848* (New York: Macmillan Publishing Co. Inc., 1974), 265.
19. Downey and Angle, 107-14.
20. Mansfield, 208.
21. Ibid., 218–19.
22. Mansfield, 311.
23. Patricia L. Faust, *Historical Times Illustrated Encyclopedia of the Civil War* (New York: Harper & Row Publishers, 1986), 790.
24, Bauer, 292.
25. Ibid., 316.
26. Downey and Angle, 134-38.
27. Mansfield, 304-20.
28. Ibid., 311.
29. Ibid., 320.

CHAPTER FOUR

1. Mansfield, *The Mexican War*, 347.
2. Weigley, *History of the United States Army*, 110.
3. Ibid., 169.
4. *Encyclopedia of American Biography, New Series* (New York: The American Historical Company, 1949), Vol. 21, 95; Mansfield, 361.

5. Mansfield, 33n.
6. Downs, 95.
7. Ibid., 95–96.
8. Cullum, *Biographical Register*, 262.
9. Grover Singley, *Tracing Minnesota's Old Government Roads* (St. Paul: Minnesota Historical Society, 1974), 1–2.
10. Jesse Lee Reno, "Report on Survey, Etc., of Road From Mendota To Big Sioux River," (33rd Congress, House Ex. Doc. No. 97, 1854), 2.
11. Ibid.
12. Ibid.
13. Ibid., 3.
14. Ibid.
15. Singley, 39–46.
16. Reno, 4.
17. Ibid., 5.
18. Singley, 40–41.
19. Ibid., 42.
20. Reno, 10.
21. Smith Pyne, letter to certify the marriage of Jesse L. Reno and Mary Cross, Military Pension Records, "Jesse L. Reno," National Archives.
22. Mary Reno, letters to Jesse Lee Reno, National Archives, Records Group 92, Entry 225, "Camp Floyd, UT."
23. Ibid.

CHAPTER FIVE

1. Norman F. Furniss, *The Mormon Conflict 1850–1859* (New Haven: Yale University Press, 1960), 67.
2. Robert S. Ellison, *Fort Bridger—A Brief History* (The Wyoming State Archives, Museums and Historical Department, 1981), 21.
3. H. K. Craig, letter order to J. L. Reno, June 25, 1857, National Archives, Records Group 92, Entry 225, "Camp Floyd, UT".
4. J. L. Reno to H. K. Craig, January 2, 1858, National Archives, Records Group 92, Entry 225, "Camp Floyd, UT".
5. Ibid.
6. Peter V. Hagner, letter to J. L. Reno, July 1, 1857, National Archives, RG 92, "Camp Floyd, UT".
7. Mary Reno, letter to Jesse Reno, July 26, 1857, National Archives, RG 92, "Camp Floyd, UT".
8. Furniss, 99–101.
9. Ibid., 99.
10. Ibid., 101.
11. Ibid., 100–112.
12. H. K. Craig, to John B. Floyd, March 22, 1858, National Archives, RG 92, "Camp Floyd, UT".
13. Stewart Sifakis, *Who Was Who in the Civil War* (New York: Facts On File Publications, 1988), 503.
14. Furniss, 101.
15. LeRoy R. Hafen and Francis Marion, *Fort Laramie and the Pageant of the West, 1834–1890* (Glendale: Arthur H. Clark Company, 1938), 285.
16. Ibid., 284.
17. Mary Reno, to Jesse Reno, August 23, 1857, National Archives, RG 92, "Camp Floyd, UT".
18. Hafen and Marion, 286.

19. Furniss, 116.
20. Ibid., 113–16; Ellison, 22.
21. Ellison, 22–23.
22. J. L. Reno, report to Craig, November 30, 1857 and January 2, 1858, National Archives, RG 92. "Camp Floyd, UT".
23. Craig to Floyd, March 22, 1858.
24. Paul Bailey, *Holy Smoke, A Dissertation on the Utah War* (Los Angeles: Westernlore Books, 1978), 106–107.
25. Reno Report to Craig, January 2, 1858.
26. Colonel A. S. Johnston's Order to J. L. Reno, April 16, 1858, National Archives, RG 92, "Camp Floyd, UT".
27. Bailey, 137.
28. Daughters of Utah Pioneers, Lesson for April, 1987, 339.
29. Robert Bardsley, "Camp Floyd, Utah and the Fairfield Inn", *True West* (October, 1987), 40.
30. Sifakis, 539–40.
31. F. J. Porter, Order to Jesse Reno, October 30, 1858, National Archives, RG 92, "Camp Floyd, UT."
32. Cullum, *Biographical Register*, 262.
33. Mary Reno, 10 Letters to Jesse L. Reno, June 27, 1857 to March 9, 1858, National Archives, Records Group 92, Entry 225, "Camp Floyd, UT".
34. *Encyclopedia of American Biography, New Series*, Vol. 21 (New York: American Historical Company, 1949), 98.

CHAPTER SIX

1. David T. Childress, "Mount Vernon Barracks: The Blue, The Gray And The Red," *Alabama Review*, Vol. 42, No. 2, (April, 1989), 128
2. Ibid., 126–27.
3. Ibid.
4. Official Records, The War of the Rebellion, Series 4, Vol. 1, 48–49. (Cited hereafter as O.R.)
5. O.R., Series 1, Vol. 1, 327.
6. O.R., Series 4, Vol. 1, 49.
7. O.R., Series 1, Vol. 1, 327.
8. E. B. Long, *The Civil War Day By Day* (Garden City: Doubleday & Company, Inc., 1971), 16.
9. George Walton, *Sentinel Of The Plains: Fort Leavenworth and the American West*, (Englewood Cliffs: Prentice-Hall, Inc., 1973), 120.
10. Willis J. Abbott, *Battle-Fields of '61* (New York: Dodd, Mead and Company, 1889), 81–87.
11. Alfred H. Guernsey and Henry M. Alden, *Harper's Pictorial History of the Civil War* (New York: Fairfax Press, 1866). Reprint, Fairfax Press, n.d., 105.
12. Walton, 120–21.
13. Ibid.
14. O.R., Series 1, Vol. 51, 373.

CHAPTER SEVEN

1. Pauline Lillie, Marengo the County Seat - Marengo the Town (Pauline Lillie in cooperation with the Marengo, Iowa-125th Celebration Committee, 1984), 173.
2. O.R., Series 1, Vol. 51, Part 1, 513.
3. Richard A. Sauers, "Laurels for Burnside: The Invasion of North Carolina, January-July 1862," *Blue & Gray Magazine*, Vol. 5, Issue 5, (May, 1988), 9.

4. Robert Underwood Johnson and Clarence Clough Buel, eds., *Battles and Leaders of the Civil War*, Vol. 1 (Secaucus, NJ: Castle, 1982), 662.
5. Willis J. Abbott, *Battle-Fields of '61* (New York: Dodd, Mead and Company, 1889), 214.
6. *National Tribune*, (Washington, D.C.: March 22, 1883).
7. Alfred H. Guernsey and Henry M. Alden, *Harper's Pictorial History of the Civil War* (New York: Fairfax Press, 1866). Reprint, Fairfax Press, 244.
8. Sauers, 11.
9. Guernsey and Alden, 245-46; Sauers, 14.
10. John Laird Wilson, *The Pictorial History of The Great Civil War* (Chicago: National Publishing Co., 1878), 126.
11. Sauers, 19.
12. Ibid., 20.
13. O.R., Series 1, Vol. 9, 99.
14. Ibid., 79.
15. *National Tribune* (Washington, D.C.: April 12, 1883).
16. O.R., Series 1, Vol. 9, 99.
17. O.R., Series 1, Vol. 9, 75.
18. *Supplement To Frank Leslie's Illustrated Newspaper* (April 5, 1862), 349.
19. Guernsey and Alden, 247.
20. Horace Greeley, *The American Conflict*, Vol. 2 of 2 vols. (Hartford: O. D. Case & Company, 1866), 78.
21. Thomas P. Kettell, *History of the Great Rebellion* (Hartford: L. Stebbins, 1865), 340.
22. Sauers, 56.
23. Rush C. Hawkins, *Battles and Leaders of the Civil War*, Vol. 1, 655.
24. O.R., Series 1, Vol. 9, 312.
25. Greeley, 79.
26. O.R., Series 1, Vol. 9, 310-13.
27. Ibid., 313-16.
28. Ibid., 307.
29. Ibid., 304.
30. Sears, *Landscape Turned Red*, 147.
31. Sifakis, *Who Was Who In The Civil War*, 295.

CHAPTER EIGHT

1. Thomas P. Kettell, *History of the Great Rebellion* (Hartford: L. Stebbins, 1865), 324.
2. John Laird Wilson, *The Pictorial History Of the Great Civil War* (Chicago: National Publishing Co., 1878), 304-305.
3. John Codman Ropes, *The Army Under Pope* (New York: Charles Scribner's Sons, 1881), 32.
4. Ibid., 32-33.
5. O.R., Series 1, Vol. 12, Part 3, 566.
6. Ropes, 33.
7. Greeley, *The American Conflict*, 180.
8. Charles Flato, *The Golden Book of the Civil War* (New York: Golden Press, 1960), 76.
9. Robert Underwood Johnson and Clarence Clough Buel, eds., *Battles and Leaders of the Civil War*, Vol. 2, 501-502.
10. Ropes, 52.
11. Flato, 76.
12. Wilson, 292-96.

13. Bruce Catton, *The American Heritage Picture History of The Civil War* (New York: American Heritage Publishing Co., 1982), 223.
14. Wilson, 300; O.R., Series 1, Vol. 12, Part 2, 43.
15. Dedication speech by Orlando B. Willcox, in C. H. Barney, ed., *The Reno Memorial* (The Society of the Burnside Expedition and the 9th Army Corps, 1891), 9.
16. Wilson, 298–99 and 304–305.
17. Johnson and Buel, *Battles and Leaders of the Civil War*, Vol. 2, 474–75.

CHAPTER NINE

1. John G. Moore, "The Battle of Chantilly," *Military Affairs,* Vol. 27, (Summer, 1964), 49.
2. Ibid., 50.
3. Patricia L. Faust, ed., *Historic Times Illustrated Encyclopedia of the Civil War* (New York: Harper & Row, 1986), 129.
4. Moore, 52–53.
5. Joseph W. A. Whitehorne, "The Battle of Chantilly," *Blue & Gray Magazine*, Vol. 4, (May, 1987), 17 & 20.
6. Moore, 59–61.
7. Vincent J. Esposito, ed., *The West Point Atlas of the Civil War* (New York: Frederick A. Praeger, 1982), Map 64.
8. Whitehorne, 52.
9. Greeley, *The American Conflict*, Vol. 2, 188.
10. O.R., Series 1, Vol. 12, Part 2, 86.
11. O.R., Series 1, Vol. 12, Part 3, 805.
12. O.R., Series 1, Vol. 51, Part 1, 782.

CHAPTER TEN

1. Faust, ed., *Historic Times Illustrated Encyclopedia of the Civil War*, 593.
2. Flato, *Golden Book of the Civil War*, 79.
3. Francis A. Lord, *They Fought For The Union* (New York: Bonanza Books, 1960), 346.
4. James M. McPherson, *Battle Cry of Freedom* (New York: Oxford University Press, 1988), 531–35.
5. John W. Schildt, *The Ninth Corps At Antietam* (Chewsville, Md., 1988), 55–56.
6. T. Harry Williams, *Hayes of the Twenty-third* (New York: Alfred A. Knopf, 1965); Charles Richard Williams, ed., *Rutherford Birchard Hayes;* Address of General E. P. Scammon, 23 Regiment, O.V.I., Annual Reunion, Lakeside, August 22, 1888, *Fremont Journal,* March 29, 1889.
7. Williams, *Hayes of the Twenty-third*, 137.
8. Williams, *Rutherford Birchard Hayes*, 348.
9. Faust, 456.
10. Williams, *Rutherford Birchard Hayes*, 195.
11. Charles F. Walcott, *History of the Twenty-First Regiment Massachusetts Volunteers* (Boston: Houghton, Mifflin, 1882), 185.
12. Sears, *Landscape Turned Red*, 147.
13. Schildt, 67.
14. Alice B. Addenbrooke, "Gen. Jesse Reno And The Flag," *Daughters of the American Revolution Magazine,* June–July, 1962, 529.
15. Conrad Reno, *General Jesse Lee Reno At Frederick* (Boston: Order of the Loyal Legion of the United States, 1900), 567–69.

CHAPTER ELEVEN

1. "The Invasion of Maryland" by James Longstreet, in *Battles and Leaders of the Civil War*, Vol. 2, 663.
2. "The Finding of Lee's Lost Order," by Silas Cosgrove, ibid., 603.
3. Steven W. Sears, "Fire On The Mountain," *Blue & Gray Magazine*, Vol. 4, January, 1987, 4.
4. Sears, *Landscape Turned Red*, 129-31.
5. Sears, *Fire On The Mountain*, 12-13.
6. John W. Schildt, *The Ninth Corps At Antietam* (Chewsville, Md., 1988), 69.
7. O.R., Series 1, Vol. 19, Part 1, 458.
8. Sears, *Fire On The Mountain*, 14.
9. Sears, *Landscape Turned Red*, 147; Schildt, 80.
10. O.R., op. cit., 48-50.
11. Longstreet, in *Battles and Leaders*, 665.
12. Forcing Fox's Gap And Turner's Gap," by Jacob D. Cox, in *Battles and Leaders*, Vol. 2, 589.
13. Charles Richard Williams, ed., *Rutherford Burchard Hayes*, Vol. 2, 195; E. P. Scammon, Address to 23 Regiment, O.V.I., Annual Reunion, Lakeside, August 22, 1888, *Fremont Journal*, March 29, 1889.
14. Oliver Christian Bosbyshell, III, *The 48th In The War* (Philadelphia: Avil Printing Company, 1893), 76.
15. Richard T. Ellis, *Leaves From The Diary of an Army Surgeon* (New York: John Bradburn, 1863), 258; *Harpers Weekly*, October 4, 1862, 634.
16. Barney, ed., *Reno Memorial*, 11.
17. Edward O. Lord, ed., *History of the Ninth Regiment New Hampshire Volunteers in the War Of The Rebellion* (Concord, N.H.: Republican Press Association, 1895), 76.
18. Barney, ed., *Reno Memorial*, 11.
19. Charles F. Walcott, *History of the Twenty-First Regiment Massachusetts Volunteers* (Boston: Houghton, Mifflin and Company, 1882), 185.
20. Francis A. Lord, *They Fought For The Union* (New York: Bonanza Books, 1960), 171-72.
21. Atlas to accompany The Official Records (Washington: Government Printing Office, 1891-1895), Plate 27, Map 3.
22. E. P. Scammon, Address to 23 Regiment, O.V.I., Annual Reunion, Lakeside, August 22, 1888, *Fremont Journal*, March 29, 1889.
23. Sears, *Landscape Turned Red*, 154-55.
24. Gabriel Campbell, Letter to Gen. Carmen, August 23, 1899, Antietam National Battlefield Site Library.
25. Gen. Ezra A. Carman, The Maryland Campaign of 1862, an unpublished, handwritten and undated manuscript in Washington County Library, Maryland. Also, letter from John B. Stickney, acting adjutant, 35 Reg. Mass. Vol., Sept. 28, 1862, Clinton H. Haskell Collection, Washington County Library.
26. A. H. Wood letter to *National Tribune*, July 26, 1883.
27. Letters to National Tribune: Henry Little and Robert West, August 9, 1883; A. B. Crummel, E. V. Richards, Matt Campbell, August 23, 1883.
28. O.R., Series 1, Vol. 21, 326.
29. O.R., Series 1, Vol. 19, Part 1, 422.
30. Ibid., 1020.
31. Ibid., 1041.
32. Walter Clark, ed., *Histories of the Several Regiments and Battalions from North Carolina in the Great War 1861-1865* (Raleigh, N.C.: N.C. Historical Commission), 221.

33. Gabriel Campbell,
34. Oliver Christian Bosbyshell, III, *The 48th In The War* (Philadelphia: Avil Printing Company, 1893), 76.

CHAPTER TWELVE

1. O.R., Series 1, Vol. 19, Part 1, 418.
2. Charles F. Walcott, *History of the Twenty-First Regiment Massachusetts Volunteers*, (Boston: Houghton, Mifflin and Company, 1882), 190-91.
3. Gen. C. H. Barney, editor, *The Reno Memorial* (Published by the Society of the Burnside Expedition and the 9th Army Corps, 1891, dedication speech by Orlando B. Willcox), 12.
4. O.R., op. cit., 27.
5. Steven R. Stotelmyer, "The Reno Monument Story," *Cracker Barrel Magazine*, September, 1989, 19.
6. Alice B. Addenbrooke, "Gen. Jesse Reno And The Flag," *Daughters of the American Revolution Magazine*, June-July, 1962, 530.
7. Conrad Reno, *General Jesse Lee Reno At Frederick* (Boston: Order of the Loyal Legion of the United States, 1900), 569.
8. Albert Nelson Marquis, editor, *Who's Who In America*, Vol. 13, 1924-1925 (Chicago: A. N. Marquis & Company), 2678.
9. Ibid.
10. Winfield Scott Downs, Litt.D., editor, *Encyclopedia of American Biography, New Series*, Vol. 21 (New York: The American Historical Company, Inc., 1949), 96-97.
11. Ibid., 97.
12. Barney, op. cit.

— BIBLIOGRAPHY

Abbott, Willis J. *Battle-Fields of '61*. New York: Dodd, Mead and Company, 1889.

Addenbrooke, Alice B. "Gen. Jesse Reno And The Flag." *Daughters of the American Revolution Magazine*, June–July, 1962.

Bailey, Paul. *Holy Smoke, A Dissertation on the Utah War*. Los Angeles: Westernlore Books, 1978.

Bardsley, Robert. "Camp Floyd, Utah and the Fairfield Inn." *True West*, October, 1987.

Barney, Gen. C. H., ed. *The Reno Memorial*. Dedication speech Orlando B. Willcox. Published by the Society of the Burnside Expedition and the 9th Army Corps, 1891.

Bauer, K. Jack. *The Mexican War 1846–1848*. New York: Macmillan Publishing Co. Inc., 1974.

Bosbyshell, Oliver Christian, III. *The 48th In The War*. Philadelphia: Avil Printing Company, 1893.

Campbell, Gabriel. Letter to Gen. Carmen, August 23, 1899. Antietam National Battlefield Site Library.

Carman, Gen. Ezra A. The Maryland Campaign of 1862. An unpublished, handwritten and undated manuscript. Washington County Library, Maryland.

Catton, Bruce. *The American Heritage Picture History of The Civil War.* New York: American Heritage Publishing Co., 1982.

Childress, David T. "Mount Vernon Barracks: The Blue, The Gray And The Red." *Alabama Review,* Vol. 42, No. 2, April, 1989.

Clark, Walter, ed. *Histories of the Several Regiments and Battalions from North Carolina in the Great War, 1861-1865.* Raleigh, N.C.: N.C. Historical Commission.

Craig, H. K. Letter to John B. Floyd, March 22, 1858. National Archives, RG 92, "Camp Floyd, UT".

——. Letter order to J. L. Reno, June 25, 1857. National Archives, RG 92, Entry 225, "Camp Floyd, UT".

Cullum, George W. *Biographical Register of the Officers and Graduates of the U.S. Military Academy.* Cambridge: Riverside Press, 1891.

Daughters of Utah Pioneers. Lesson for April, 1987. Pioneer Museum. Salt Lake City, Utah.

Downey, Fairfax, and Paul Angle. *Texas and the War With Mexico.* New York: American Heritage Publishing Co. Inc., 1961.

Downs, Winfield Scott, Litt.D., ed. *Encyclopedia of American Biography, New Series,* Vol. 21. New York: The American Historical Company, Inc. 1949.

Ellis, Richard T. *Leaves From The Diary of an Army Surgeon.* New York: John Bradburn, 1863.

Ellison, Robert S. *Fort Bridger—A Brief History.* The Wyoming State Archives, Museums and Historical Department, 1981.

Esposito, Vincent J., ed. *The West Point Atlas of the Civil War.* New York: Frederick A. Praeger, 1982.

Faust, Patricia L., ed. *Historic Times Illustrated Encyclopedia of the Civil War.* New York: Harper & Row, 1986.

Flato, Charles. *The Golden Book of the Civil War.* New York: Golden Press, 1960.

Franklin, Pennsylvania Public Library. Newspaper clipping file: "Reno".

Furniss, Norman F. *The Mormon Conflict 1850-1859.* New Haven: Yale University Press, 1960.

Greeley, Horace. *The American Conflict.* Vol. 2. Hartford: O. D. Case & Company, 1866.

Guernsey, Alfred H., and Henry M. Alden. *Harper's Pictorial History of the Civil War.* New York: Fairfax Press, 1866. Fairfax Press, reprint, n.d.

Hafen, LeRoy R., and Francis Marion. *Fort Laramie and the Pageant of the West, 1834-1890.* Glendale: Arthur H. Clark Company, 1938.

Hagner, Peter V. Letter to J. L. Reno, July 1, 1857. National Archives, RG 92, "Camp Floyd, UT".

Harpers Weekly. New York, October 4, 1862.

History of Venango County, Pennsylvania, 1879. Reprint, Venango County Historical Society, Franklin, Pa., 1976.

History of Venango County, Pennsylvania, 1890. Reprint, Venango County Historical Society, Franklin, Pa., 1984.

Johnson, Robert Underwood, and Clarence Clough Buel, eds. *Battles and Leaders of the Civil War.* Vols. 1 & 2. Secaucus, N.J.: Castle, 1982.

Johnston, Colonel A. S. Order to J. L. Reno, April 16, 1858. National Archives, RG 92, "Camp Floyd, UT".

Kettell, Thomas P. *History of the Great Rebellion.* Hartford: L. Stebbins, 1865.

Leslie, Frank. *Frank Leslie's Illustrated Newspaper, Supplement,* April 5, 1862.

Lillie, Pauline. Marengo the County Seat - Marengo the Town. Written in cooperation with the Marengo, Iowa 125th Celebration Committee, 1984.

Long, E. B. *The Civil War Day By Day.* Garden City: Doubleday & Company, Inc., 1971.

Lord, Edward O., ed. *History of the Ninth Regiment New Hampshire Volunteers in the War Of The Rebellion.* Concord, N.H.: Republican Press Association, 1895.

Lord, Francis A. *They Fought For The Union.* New York: Bonanza Books, 1960.

Mansfield, Edward D. *The Mexican War.* New York: A. S. Barnes & Co., 1858.

Marquis, Albert Nelson, ed. *Who's Who In America.* Vol. 13., 1924-1925. Chicago: AN Marquis & Company.

McPherson, James M. *Battle Cry of Freedom.* New York: Oxford University Press, 1988.

Moore, John G. "The Battle of Chantilly." Military Affairs. Vol. 27. Summer, 1964.

National Tribune. Washington, D.C. March 22, April 12, July 26, August 9 and August 23, 1883.

Porter, F. J. Order to Jesse Reno, October 30, 1858. National Archives, RG 92, "Camp Floyd, UT".

Pyne, Smith. Letter to certify marriage of Jesse L. Reno and Mary Cross. National Archives, Military Pension Records, "Jesse L. Reno".

Reno, Conrad. General Jesse Lee Reno At Frederick. Boston: Order of the Loyal Legion of the United States, 1900.

Reno, Jesse Lee. "Report on Survey, Etc., of Road From Mendota to Big Sioux River." 33rd Congress, House Doc. No. 97, 1854.

——. Notarized statement of Mexican War Service, October 31, 1850. Made for purpose of securing bounty land. National Archives, Pension Records.

——. Reports to H. K. Craig, November 30, 1857 and January 2, 1858. National Archives, RG 92, "Camp Floyd, UT".

Reno, Mary. Ten letters to Jesse L. Reno, June 28, 1857 to March 9, 1858. National Archives, RG 92, Entry 225, "Camp Floyd, UT".

Reno, Roger, Rockford, Ill., and William L. Reno, Falls Church, Va. Extensive unpublished Reno family genealogical information.

Ropes, John Codman. The Army Under Pope. New York: Charles Scribner's Sons, 1881.

Sauers, Richard A. "Laurels for Burnside: The Invasion of North Carolina, January–July 1862." Blue & Gray Magazine. Vol. 5, issue 5, May, 1988.

Scammon, E. P. Address to 23 Regiment, O.V.I. Annual Reunion, Lakeside, August 22, 1888. Fremont Journal, March 29, 1889.

Schildt, John W. The Ninth Corps At Antietam. Chewsville, Md., 1988.

Schubert, Frank N. Vanguard of Expansion. Washington: Government Printing Office, 1980.

Sears, Steven W. Landscape Turned Red. New York: Popular Library, 1985.

——. "Fire On The Mountain," Blue & Gray Magazine. Vol. 4, January, 1987.

Sifakis, Stewart. Who Was Who in the Civil War. New York: Facts On File Publications, 1988.

Singley, Grover. *Tracing Minnesota's Old Government Roads.* St. Paul, Minnesota Historical Society, 1974.

Stickney, John B., acting adjutant. 35 Reg. Mass. Vol., Letter to parents, Sept. 28, 1862. Clinton H. Haskell Collection, Washington County Library, Md.

Stotelmyer, Steven R. "The Reno Monument Story," *Cracker Barrel Magazine*, September, 1989.

Universal Standard Encyclopedia. Vol. 20. New York: Standard Reference Works Publishing Co., Inc., 1958.

U.S. Military Academy Archives. Cadet Delinquency Record. West Point, NY.

——. Post Order Book #2, Special Orders 107 & 119.

U.S. War Department. Instruction For Mountain Howitzers, prepared by a board of army officers, 1851. Washington: Gibbon & Co.

——. War of the Rebellion: A Compilation of the Official Records of the Union and Confederate Armies. 128 vols. Washington: Government Printing Office, 1880–1901.

——. Atlas to Accompany The Official Records. Washington: Government Printing Office, 1891–1895.

Utley, Robert M. *Frontiersmen in Blue.* Lincoln: University of Nebraska Press, 1967.

Walcott, Charles F. *History of the Twenty-First Regiment Massachusetts Volunteers.* Boston: Houghton, Mifflin and Company, 1882.

Walton, George. *Sentinel Of The Plains: Fort Leavenworth and the American West.* Englewood Cliffs, N.J.: Prentice-Hall, Inc., 1973.

Weigley, Russell F. *History of the United States Army.* Bloomington: Indiana University Press, 1984.

Whitehorne, Joseph W. A. "The Battle of Chantilly." *Blue & Gray Magazine.* Vol. 4, May, 1987.

Williams, Charles Richard. *Rutherford Birchard Hayes.* Vol. 2. Boston: Houghton, Mifflin and Company, 1914.

Williams, T. Harry. *Hayes of the Twenty-third.* New York: Alfred A. Knopf, 1965.

Wilson, John Laird. *The Pictorial History of the Great Civil War.* Chicago: National Publishing Co., 1878.

Winter, Frank H., and Mitchell R. Sharp. "Major Lion's Rocketeers: The New York Rocket Battalion," *Civil War Times Illustrated.* Vol. 11, No. 9, January, 1973.

— _Index_

A

Albemarle Sound, N.C., 50-51, 53
Alexander, Col. Edmund B., 26-29
Alexandria, Va., 65, 69
Allegheny Arsenal (Pittsburgh), 25
Allegheny College, Pa., 3
Annapolis, Md., 42-43, 45-46
Antietam, Md., 77
Aquia Creek, 59
Army of Northern Virginia, C.S.A., 76
Army of Virginia, U.S.A., 57, 59
Arsenals
   Allegheny, 25
   Frankford, 22-25, 30, 32-33
   Leavenworth, 41
   Mount Vernon, 36-39
   St. Louis, 25
   Watervliet, 9
Artillery units
   Battery C, 3rd Artillery, 26, 28, 30
Artillery, use of, 8-9, 12-14

B

Barbara Fritchie flag, 73-75, 89
Battles. _See under_ Bull Run, Chantilly,
   New Bern, South Mountain
Beanes, Dr. William B., 17
Beaufort, N.C., 52
Bennett, Sgt. Charles W., 86
Big Sioux River, 18-20

Birney, Brig. Gen. David B., 68
Boonsboro, Md., 78
Boston, Mass., 89
Branch, Brig. Gen. Lawrence O., 51
Brevet rank, 14, 16
Buchanan, President James, 24, 29
Bull Run, 1-2
Bull Run, Second Battle of, 56-57, 59-
   65
Burgwyn, Lt. Col. William S., 50
Burnside, Brig. Gen. (later Maj. Gen.)
   Ambrose E.
   early career, 41-45, 47-48, 50
   in North Carolina, 51-52, 54-55
   as commander, IX Corps, 59, 70, 80,
      82-83, 88
Burnside's expedition, 43, 45-55

C

Camp Floyd, Utah, 30
Camp Scott, Utah, 28
Camp Winfield, Utah, 28
Campbell, Capt. Gabriel, 86-87
Cape Hatteras, N.C., 46
Castle of Chapultepec. _See_ Chapultepec
Cedar Mountain, battle of, 57
Centreville, Va., 64-65
Cerro Gordo, battle of, 12-13
Chantilly, battle of, 59, 61, 66, 68-69
Chapultepec, battle of, 14

Church of Jesus Christ of Latter Day Saints, 24. *See also* Mormons
Churubusco, battle of, 14
Clark, Gov. Henry T. (S.C.), 47
Class of 1846, U.S. Military Academy, 4-8
Coastal Division, 42-43, 50. *See also* Burnside expedition
Confederate States Army units
  3rd Georgia, 53
  8th North Carolina, 47
  23rd North Carolina, 86
  31st North Carolina, 49
Corps of Topographical Engineers, 18, 22
Council Bluffs, Iowa, 18
Cox, Brig. Gen. Jacob D., 79-80
Craig, Col. Henry, 24-25, 28-29
Cross (surveyor), 18, 20-21
Cross, Eliza Bradley Beanes (mother-in-law), 17
Cross, Mary Bradley Beanes (Mrs. Jesse Lee Reno), 17-18, 21-22. *See also* Reno, Mary Cross
Cross, Col. Trueman (father-in-law), 17
Cross, William (brother-in-law), 33-34
Culpeper Court House, Va., 57
Cutter, Dr. Calvin, 81, 85

D

Davis, Secretary of War Jefferson, 21-22
Derby, George H., 5-6
Dismal Swamp Canal, 52, 54
Drexler, C., 29

E

El Reno, Okla., 96
Elizabeth City, N.C., 53
Erie, Pa., 4, 16

F

Fairfax Court House, Va., 65
Fecken, Martin, 85
Ferrero, Brig. Gen. (later Maj. Gen.) Edward, 85
Floyd, Secretary of War John B., 28-29, 39
Fort Bridger, Wyo., 27-28
Fort Kearney, Neb., 27
Fort Laramie, Wyo., 27
Fort Leavenworth, Kansas, 23-27, 39, 40-41, 43

Fort Macon, N.C., 52
Fort Monroe, Va., 45-46, 55
Foster, Brig. Gen. John G., 41, 43, 48-52
Fox's Gap (South Mountain), 79-80
Frankford Arsenal (Philadelphia), 22-25, 30, 32-33
Franklin, Pa., 2-4
Frederick, Md., 71, 73-78
Fritchie, Barbara, 73, 75, 89

G

Germantown, Va., 65-66
Gibbon, Maj. Gen. John, 62
Goldsborough, Louis, 46-47
Gorgas, Maj. Josiah, 36-37
Gorgas, William C., 37
Grant, Maj. Gen. Ulysses S., 8, 14
Great Salt Lake, Utah, 24

H

Hagner, Bvt. Maj. Peter V., 15, 22-23, 25, 39
Halleck, Maj. Gen. Henry W., 57
Hampton Roads, Va., 46
Harney, Brig. Gen. William S., 26
Harpers Ferry, Va., 76-77
Hatteras Inlet, N.C., 46-47, 59
Hawkins, Col. Rush, 49, 51-55
Hawkins' Zouaves. *See* 9th New York
Hayes, Lt. Col. Rutherford B., 71-73, 83
Hill, Maj. Gen. Daniel H., 2, 79, 86, 89
Hooker, Maj. Gen. Joseph, 66
Howitzers. *See* mountain howitzers

I

Indians, 19-20, 26-27. *See also* Minnesota expedition

J

Jackson, Gov. Claiborne (Mo.), 40
Jackson, Maj. Gen. Thomas J. "Stonewall", 6, 57, 59-62, 64-66, 73, 76, 84-85, 89
James, Chaplain Horace, 50
Johnston, Bvt. Brig. Gen. Albert Sidney, 23, 27-30
Jordan, Col. J. K., 49

K

Kalapaza, John N., 25
Kearney, Maj. Gen. Philip, 61-62, 68
Kinston, N.C., 86

L

Lee, Gen. Robert E., 8, 12, 57, 59-62, 64-65
  in Maryland campaign, 71, 76-79
Liberty, Mo., 39-41
Lincoln, President Abraham, 45, 56-57, 63, 70
Little River Turnpike, Va., 65-66, 69
Little Sioux River, 18
Longstreet, Maj. Gen. James, 57, 61-62, 76, 80
Lost Order, 78-79

Mc

McClellan, Maj. Gen. George B., 5, 8, 41-43, 56-57, 62-63, 69, 89
  in Maryland campaign, 70-71, 73, 76-80
McRae, Col. D. K., 86

M

Maggi, Lt. Col. Alberto, 49
Manassas, battle of. *See* Bull Run
Manassas Junction, Va., 60-61
Mankato, Minn., 20-21
Marengo, Iowa, 4
Maryland campaign, 70-71, 73, 75-82
Mendota, Minn., 18, 20-21
Mexico City, Mexico, 10, 12-14
Middletown, Md., 79
Miles, Col. Dixon S., 41
Minnesota surveying expedition, 18-21
Mississippi River, 18
Missouri River, 18-19
Mitchell, Cpl. Burton W., 77-78
Mobile, Ala., 36, 38
Moore, Gov. Andrew B. (Ala.), 38
Mormons, 24, 26-30
Mountain howitzers, 9-10, 12-14
Mount Vernon Arsenal (Ala.), 36-39

N

Nag's Head, N.C., 46-47
Neuse River, 51
New Bern, N.C., 50-52
Norfolk, Va., 52, 54
North Carolina campaign, 42, 45-55

O

Oak Hill Cemetery, Georgetown, D.C., 91, 95
Ordnance Corps, 7, 9, 17-18, 22-23

P

Parke, Brig. Gen. John G., 41, 43, 47-48, 50-52, 55
Pasquotank River, 52-53
Peninsula campaign, 56-57
Phelps, Capt. John W., 26
Pickett, (later Maj. Gen.) George E., 5
Pleasonton, Brig. Gen. Alfred, 78-79
Pope, Maj. Gen. John, 56, 59-66, 69-70
Porter, Maj. Gen. Fitz-John, 61-62
Puebla, Mexico, 13-14

R

Rapidan River, 57
Rappahannock River, 57, 59, 64
Reno, Alexander (son), 30, 34, 36, 95
Reno, Benjamin Franklin (brother), 4, 43, 50, 75, 86, 89
Reno, Charles (grandfather), 2
Reno, Conrad (son), 30, 37, 95
Reno, Frances Laughlin (grandmother), 2
Reno, Maj. Gen. Jesse Lee, x-xi
  family background, 1-3
  West Point years, 4-7
  during War with Mexico, 8-10, 13-15
  in peacetime army, 16-22
  on Mormon expedition, 24-30
  family life of, 31-35
  in the South, 36-39
  at Fort Leavenworth, 40-41
  North Carolina campaign, 41-43, 45-46, 48-55
  2nd Bull Run, 56, 59-63
  at Chantilly, 64-66, 68-69
  during Maryland campaign, 70-75, 78-81
  death of, 81-87
  remembrances of, 88-89, 95-96
Reno, Jesse Wilford (son), 41, 95
Reno, Lewis (immigrant to U.S.), 1-2
Reno, Lewis (brother), 4
Reno, Lewis (son), 22-23, 25, 27, 32-34, 95
Reno, Lewis Thomas (father), 2, 4
Reno, Marian (daughter), 22, 95
Reno, Mary Cross (wife), 22-23, 25, 27. *See also* Cross, Mary
  letters of, 30-35
  at army posts, 36-37, 41
  memorials for her husband, 89-90, 95
Reno, Rebecca Quinby (mother), 2, 4

Reno, Nev., 96
Reno, Pa., 4-5
Reno's battery, 13-15
Reynaud, Lewis. *See* Reno, Lewis (immigrant)
Reynolds, Bvt. Maj. (later Maj. Gen.) John F., 30
Richmond, Va., 42, 47, 56-57
Road surveying, 18-21
Roanoke Island, N.C., 42, 46-52, 54, 86. *See also* Burnside expedition
Robinson, Gov. Charles (Kansas), 40
Rockets, 9
Rowan, Commodore Stephen Clegg, 52

S

St. John's Episcopal Church, 21-22, 34
St. Louis, Mo., 18, 25
St. Paul, Minn., 20-21
Salt Lake City, Utah, 28-30
Santa Anna, Gen. Antonio Lopez de, 9, 12-14
Scammon, Col. Eliakim P., 72, 80-81
Scott, Cyrus, 19
Scott, Gen. Winfield, 8-10, 15, 41
Second Dragoons, 26
Shaw, Col. H. M., 47
Sibley, Henry Hastings, 18
Sioux City, Iowa, 18, 20
South Mills, N.C., 52-54
South Mountain, battle of, 73, 77-79, 88, 96
Special Order No. 191, 78. *See also* lost order
Stanton, Secretary of War Edwin M., 55
Steele, Capt. William, 40
Stevens, Maj. Gen. Isaac, 65-66, 68
Stoneman, Brig. Gen. George, 6-7
Stuart, Maj. Gen. James E. B. "Jeb", 65-66, 78
Sturgis, Brig. Gen. Samuel D., 6, 81

T

Taylor, Gen. Zachary, 10, 12
Tilton, James, 18, 21
Trent River, 52
Twiggs, Bvt. Maj. Gen. David E., 12-13

U

United States Army units
Regular Army
5th Infantry, 26
10th Infantry, 26
IX Corps, 66, 68, 70-71, 73, 78, 80, 84
10th Connecticut, 45
27th Indiana, 77
2nd Iowa Cavalry, 43
21st Massachusetts, 43, 46, 49, 51-54, 83, 88-89
24th Massachusetts, 50
25th Massachusetts, 45
17th Michigan, 86
20th Michigan, 85-86
6th New Hampshire, 43, 45, 47, 53-54
9th New Jersey, 43
9th New York (Hawkins' Zouaves), 47, 49, 51, 53-54
51st New York, 43
79th New York, 66
89th New York, 53
23rd Ohio, 71-73, 80, 83-84
51st Pennsylvania, 43-44, 52-54
United States Military Academy, 3, 7. *See also* West Point
Utah expedition, 24-30

V

Valley View, Va., 2-3, 34
Vera Cruz, Mexico, 10, 12
Voltigeurs, 13-15

W

War with Mexico, 8-10, 12-15
Warrenton Pike, Va., 65-66, 68
Washington, D.C., 17, 21-22, 30, 33, 37, 43, 56, 71, 90
Watervliet Arsenal (New York), 9
West Point, 59, 64, 72. *See also* United States Military Academy
Reno at, 3-7, 16-17
Wheeling, (West) Va., 2
Whittier, John Greenleaf, 73-75
Willcox, Maj. Gen. Orlando B., 5-6, 62, 83, 87, 96
Winchester, Va., 2
Wise, Brig. Gen. Henry A., 47, 50
Wise, Capt. O. Jennings, 50
Wood, Sergeant A. H., 85-86
Wright, Col. Ambrose, 53

Y

Young, Brigham, 24, 29